TRAINING THAT MAKES SENSE

A.J. Kirshner

Academic Therapy Publications
San Rafael, California

Standard Book Number: 0-87879-034-9
Library of Congress Catalog Card Number: 77-188850

Foreword by Marshall McLuhan, copyright 1971,
McLuhan Associates Limited.

PRINTED IN THE UNITED STATES OF AMERICA

Academic Therapy Publications
San Rafael, California

CONTENTS

To Eleanor

who showed us the way by her life of quiet dignity and courage.

FOREWORD

Many of the basic percepts that are so effectively put in play in the perceptual training procedures of A. J. Kirshner came to attention in the educational practices of Maria Montessori. She, in turn, had understood the unusual developments in the experimental arts of her time. The later nineteenth century had developed a concensus concerning the need for a unified sensibility. The specialisms of Romantic sentiment and their dispersal in picturesque landscape modes, seemed suddenly to converge in a general demand for the union of thought and feeling, of emotion and involvement in creative process. The breakthrough of Max Planck into a new physics, in 1900, seemed to prepare a beachhead for many endeavors in the arts and sciences, in physics and in music and painting alike.

It was in 1893 that Adolf Hildebrand, the sculptor, published *The Problem of Form in Painting and Sculpture* (N.Y.: G. E. Stechert and Co.), in which he presented the principles of visual training and perception that changed many older approaches to art and education. His theme is radical: "Nature having endowed our eyes so richly, these two functions of seeing and touching exist here in a far more intimate union than they do when performed by different sense organs. An artistic talent consists in having these two functions precisely and harmoniously related."

Increasingly, the idea of a natural and creatively integrated life has become accepted as the *effect* of well-developed sensory perception. Any distortion or bias in the nourishment received by our senses has now been recognized as the cause of defective learning and impoverished impulse. Hildebrand had already in 1893 seen that the educational stress must shift from the mere diet to involvement in the actual *process* of assimilation and control: "Since Art does not depend upon a mere *knowing* but on a *doing* which puts this knowledge into practice, a treatise on artistic problems can be fruitful only when it follows the artistic process in its practical as well as in its theoretical aspects." The approach both to art and learning had suddenly shifted from mere consumerism and appreciation to participation in the actual process of making: "Art can flourish only when the artist follows the natural paths of production. Let him, then, get his result, however modest, by natural means, rather than to strive to achieve something more brilliant, the outcome of a greater ability than he possesses."

By fidelity to the actual process of perceiving and making, Hildebrand entered a realm of spatial form that is prophetic of the approach to perceptual training now explored and presented in Kirshner's perceptual-motor training: "The sculptor's specific mental material consists in kinesthetic ideas. To these he gives expression by fashioning them out with his hands in solid material . . . . For it does not follow that forms which are expressive when perceived by touch at close range, should continue to be so when presented in the visual projection."

Hildebrand is insisting not on illusion but on a togetherness of the senses, a sensory interface as a means of validating impressions of space and form: "We see, therefore, that both sculptor and painter have to deal with the relation existing between visual impressions and kinesthetic ideas." It is on a vast experience of touch and motion from which, in fact, we derive our ideas of form: "It is obtained either through movement direct, or is inferred from the appearance not only of the object's actual form, but of the illumination, the environment and the changing point of view."

Hildebrand moves easily and casually into the heart of the learning problem by indicating the crux as a sort of "total field" pattern. He, as it were, anticipates Kirshner's current work by telling us how the most advanced artistic perception of 1893 coincides with recent developments in learning theory and practice. Neither Hildebrand nor Kirshner can be outmoded because both take their stand on the *figure* of the learner in relation to the environmental *ground*. The interplay *between* these forms is where the action is, and neither can have its meaning or effect alone: "By conceiving Nature as a relation of kinesthetic ideas to visual impressions, all combined and interrelated in a totality, Art frees her of change and chance." It follows that for both learner and environment, for *figure* and *ground*, that any change in the proportions of either creates "a new ball game" for everybody.

Like Edgar Allan Poe, Hildebrand saw that the new electric speed of intercommunication resulting from the telegraph imposed a new pattern of awareness of the end preceding the beginning, as if both were always *now*. Just as Poe recognized that a work of art must begin with the effect to be attained, Hildebrand could say: "In true Art the actual form has its reality only as an effect." Today in education also, training begins with the effect to be achieved, for it is only by involvement in the process itself that awareness and mastery occur. We learn to walk and talk by making as if we could walk and talk.

The Kirshner Arrows and Fingers charts in Chapter 3, "Integration," provide the child with instant musical experience—where "the end precedes the beginning." Children learn to read notation and respond with speech and movement to an acoustic environment, without prior learning.

In education today we are acutely conscious of the failure of packaged fare for the young. Hildebrand helps us to make the further necessary step of exploiting not the connections between concepts but the *intervals* of time and space between the components of the educational process. It is the play between the wheel and the axle that constitute wheel and axle. To keep in touch there must be an interval in art as in life in order that there be perception, dialogue, and discovery. Interplay leads to the resonance that brings discovery in all directions. What Buckminster Fuller calls "omni-directional" space is the

360-degree world of the auditory and acoustic experience in which we live as much as fish in water, and just as unaware. Kirshner's kinesthetic program for integrating and expanding our sensory lives also affords the means of uniting the visual and auditory imagination of the child.

Marshall McLuhan, Director

Centre For Culture and Technology
University of Toronto
Canada

ACKNOWLEDGMENTS

Among the many who have contributed to the ideas presented in this book, I wish to express my appreciation to Mr. S. B. Montin, Director of Special Services for the Protestant School Board of Greater Montreal, and Miss P. Steel, Principal of Herbert Symonds School, for their contributions to the experimental program for twenty students discussed in Chapter 6. The research was supported in part by a grant from the Medical Research Council 297-39, directed by Dr. S. Z. Dudek.

In Chapter 1, the section entitled "The Bright Boy Who Could Not Get Promoted" is based on an article which appeared in the *Quebec Home and School News*, December 1963, and I gratefully acknowledge their permission to include it in this book. I have also drawn upon some of my previously published papers, expanding them in the light of additional work and research.

Photos of the Kirshner Body Alphabet have been provided through the courtesy of Mafex Associates, Johnstown, Pennsylvania.

Most grateful appreciation is extended to the many children with whom I have worked over the years—a few of them appear in this book. (The children in the illustrations do not have handicaps; they simply posed for the pictures.) All of the children are greatly responsible for the practical approach of this book—they have taught me the importance of *Training that Makes Sense*.

A. J. Kirshner

INTRODUCTION:
TRAINING THAT MAKES SENSE

This is a book on perceptual-motor training for exceptional children. I am aware that there is a great volume of literature on this subject. Why then another book? Because this field of child care is relatively new, and because much of the training takes into account the physiological structure of the child and is often movement centered *but without much meaning*.

I have had many years of experience in providing children with optometric visual therapy to bring about better functioning of the visual processes. Training was given in oculomotor skills, binocular vision, eye-hand coordination, body image, space awareness, and intermodal integration. It soon became apparent that in order to maintain the interest of the child, I would have to translate the program into games. Hence, the title of this book on sensorimotor training: *Training That Makes Sense.*

I am indebted to M. S. Rabinovitch, psychologist, and Clifford Kolson, reading specialist, who encouraged my work with children long before my theories were formulated. Since the theories grew out of the practice, this book has been organized to begin with the case histories of the children who taught me the principles. Whenever there is any conflict between theory and practice, I resolve it in the words of Joseph Wepman: "If you are interested in theories of behavior, then study theories—not children."

This book cannot be used in a rigid, pedantic manner. It takes the warmth and imagination of a good teacher to bring the ideas to life. After thirty years of experience with children, I do not have a set formula for programing the training. I do not begin training each child in the same way, nor do I proceed to new levels according to a strict methodology. I am concerned when we commence a program and always surprised and delighted when the child improves. David Kretch expressed his feelings about the vastness of the study of the child when he said, "The understanding of atomic physics is child's play compared to the understanding of child's play."

A. J. Kirshner

A. J. KIRSHNER, O.D., is consultant to the Learning Clinic of McGill University and the Montreal Children's Hospital. He is lecturer in the Department of Ortho-pedagogie, University of Sherbrooke. He has worked in the field of Developmental Reading at Sir George Williams University, Massachusetts Institute of Technology, and Hebrew University. Dr. Kirshner is a graduate of the School of Optometry and director of the Visual Motor Training Center, University of Montreal.

Chapter 1. THREE CHILDREN WITH PROBLEMS

In chapter I you will meet three children who represent a wide spectrum of children in difficulty.

Jimmy, the bright boy who could not get promoted, can be found in every classroom in the world. He is bright, has good language development, and should be a good scholar. He has difficulty in concentrating, he makes "careless" mistakes in reading, and he is often mistaken as undermotivated.

David, the boy who wouldn't talk, is the autistic child with poor language development. The program of sensorimotor training developed for David can be used in schools for retarded children.

Alice, the girl who talked too much, the emotionally disturbed girl with a severe body image disturbance, recovered dramatically when her body image was developed.

At the time when these children were seen (1949 to 1960), there was no therapy that would meet their specific needs. The main diagnostic and remedial procedures grew out of my attempts to solve the problems presented by these three children.

THE BRIGHT BOY WHO COULD NOT GET PROMOTED

I first became aware of the vast potential of optometric visual training in the field of learning in August of 1949. The director of physical education of McGill University referred Jimmy for testing because he was unable to pass grade eight after two attempts. Jimmy was examined by a psychologist, a psychiatrist, and an eye specialist. They could find no reason for his failure.

The psychologist recommended that in view of the school difficulty Jimmy should study farming or animal husbandry. This came as a severe blow to his parents; they had always expected to send their only son to a university.

Jimmy's home was rich in culture and intellectual stimulation; his father, a statistician, and his mother, a former school teacher, had provided the kind of home that fosters high scholarship. The psychologist was quick to point out that Jimmy had sufficient intelligence for the university level, but that he was unable to mobilize himself for academic work.

In September Jimmy was reenrolled in the same school and he commenced his visual training after school. Within a short time Jimmy's parents noticed an improvement in his concentration and reading ability. When the training was completed in December of the same year, the teacher reported that Jimmy was making satisfactory grades in all subjects. In 1953 Jimmy completed his high school training and was accepted in a university.

What Happened to Jimmy?

That was what everyone was asking Jimmy's parents; he was so changed! "Jimmy's two sisters used to push him around and tease him; he soon put a stop to all that," said his mother. "He can now play baseball and football with the boys in the neighborhood. It has made such a difference!"

Optometrists who used visual training to improve the control and coordination of the eyes often found that their patients made significant gains in school. This was puzzling because the optometrists could not understand the mechanism that brought about the school improvement. In order to find out why so many children were being helped by visual training, G. N. Getman, an optometrist from Luverne, Minnesota, joined the staff of the Gesell Institute of Child Development in 1946 to study the role of vision in child growth. He made daily measurements of vision and he observed how vision was integrated into the child behavior.

A. Gesell, L. B. Ames, F. R. Ilg, G. Bullis, and G. N. Getman studied the implication of the vision findings and together they arrived at a principle that was to greatly expand our concept of helping the child with a learning problem: *Seeing is not a separate function; seeing is integrated into the total action (muscular) system of the child.* When the integration between seeing and action was incomplete, the patient had a visual-motor problem that could interfere with school success. The combined researches of optometry, psychology and child development led to visual-motor training as we know it today.

What Is a Visual-Motor Problem?

All the eye specialists agree that it is not an eye problem. Jimmy had 20/20 vision in each eye, no short sight, astigmatism, or farsight. There was no evidence of any eye disease. The basic meaning of a visual-motor problem is that the child has difficulty in seeing (vision) and doing (motor). When Jimmy was asked to copy a series of simple shapes, such as circles, squares, and diamonds, he was in trouble. He could not match the *seeing* with the *doing*.

When Jimmy was asked to read aloud, he left out words and endings and he read in a halting voice. Jimmy's handwriting was poor and his art work discouraging. This demonstrates difficulty in the *doing* part of his system. Students with visual-motor problems cannot reproduce what they see. They are better in oral than in written work. They are said to have poor eye-hand coordination.

Eye-hand coordination is a very complex process that involves more than just moving muscles. In order to draw a picture, the child must steer his hand through a complicated path. In order to steer the hand, he must know exactly where it is in space; then he must plan his movement so that his hand executes what his eyes perceive. Jimmy and children with perceptual-motor problems are not quite sure of where their limbs are. Imagine trying to steer a car with a dirty windshield; unless you can see precisely where the car is located on the road, driving can be very dangerous. Knowledge of where the body is in space is called the *body image*. Jimmy had poor body image.

Here is the evidence. Suppose we ask Jimmy to draw a diamond (Figure 1). He draws a line from A to B without difficulty; he draws the next line from B to C, but unfortunately he goes too far because he did not know that his hand had passed the point just above A. From C to D he realizes that he will not make a diamond unless he curves outward to D. When he tries to draw the line from D to A, he cannot plan the movement and he goes past A before he realizes his mistake, then he curves back and makes the characteristic "hump" which shows that he does not know where his hands are and cannot steer them adequately. Imagine Jimmy's problem when the teacher asks him to write or draw a map.

FIGURE 1. Jimmy's Drawing of a Diamond Shape

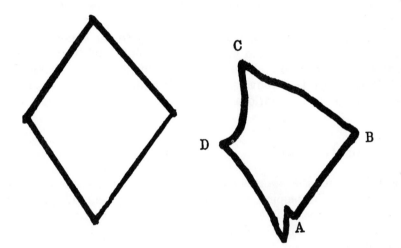

The inadequate body image for hand movements also exists when Jimmy is asked to move his eyes. At first he will move his head when he tries to follow a moving target, showing that he has more control of his neck muscles that move the head than the small muscles that move the eyes.

When we ask Jimmy not to move his head, his eyes make erratic movements when following a circular path (Figure 2). Jimmy cannot keep his eyes on his book; he frequently loses his place and thus misreads words or reads in a slow, halting manner.

Why is control of the eyes so important for school work? In order to understand this, it is necessary to know the relationship between eye and brain. W. S. McCulloch, neurophysiologist of Massachusetts Institute of Technology, states that "Each eye is capable of supplying as much information to the brain as does the rest of the body."[1]   H. F. R. Prechtl, chief of the department of experimental neurology, University of Groningen, Holland, states, "A group of 50 children who had behavior disorders and school difficulty were given extensive neurological tests; 96 percent of this group had poor eye movements in addition to poor control of other groups of muscles. We could record errors in word recognition with occurrence of involuntary eye movements by recording an electro-oculogram during reading. It seems sensible to suppose that difficulty in fixation may lead to considerable functional disturbance."[2]

FIGURE 2. Path of Jimmy's Eye Following Circular Movement

Thus we can see that a child who cannot adequately control his eyes will have difficulty in keeping a large area of brain on the task. This results in short attention span. Young children exhibit the perceptual-motor problem long before they reach school. The nursery school teacher notes how they do not wish to color and draw; they rarely stay more than a few minutes at any task, and these children are seen running from one activity to the other without pattern or purpose. In kindergarten and grade one they continue to do poor work in their workbooks and in art—all this is in spite of normal intelligence and the ability to hold interesting conversations with adults who find them to be very knowledgeable about the world around them.

Visual-Motor Training

What brought about the improvement that was to change Jimmy's life and give him a future more in keeping with his intellectual potential? In the training program it seemed reasonable to proceed along the path of development taken by the growing child. The Gesell chart of child development shows the following stages of growth:

4 weeks	Ocular Control
16 weeks	Head Balance
28 weeks	Hand Grasp and Manipulation
40 weeks	Finger Control

Thus the training emphasized control of the eyes: widening of the span of vision so that the student may see more at a single glance; improving the control of hands by commencing with large rhythmic movements and later introducing small movements and fine control of fingers; and then interweaving hand and eye activities such as ball bouncing, target shooting, model building, and exercises to improve body balance.

When Jimmy had developed better body image that enabled him to skillfully control his movements, when he developed better control of his eyes, he was able to maintain his attention for long periods of time on his reading and visual task. He suddenly found school work much easier and he was able to use his intellectual gifts.

Just as a child may have a language problem and still have normal hearing when tested on an audiometer with pure tones, so a child with a visual-motor problem may have perfect vision (20/20) when he is tested on a Snellen Chart. Both of these children have difficulty in the interpretation of the sound or light stimuli that gives meaning to the language symbols either in print (reading) or in hearing (language). Further research to help school children towards better learning will come from many professions working together.

THE STORY OF DAVID—THE BOY WHO WOULD NOT TALK

Early in 1957, the director of the Children's Hospital, department of psychology, referred David, age six. I was cautioned, "You had better tie down everything in your office or David will wreck it." David's history showed that he was of premature birth; he had suffered anoxia and was placed in an incubator. His language development was delayed; there was slow motor development; he was impulsive, infantile, and he rejected the affection of his parents and siblings. It was not possible to perform any of the standard psychological tests because of his short attention span and destructive behavior. When David was two years old, the parents were advised by a medical consultant to place him in an institution. They sought the counsel of a psychologist who, sensing the parents' deep attachment to their deviant child, recommended that they keep him—that perhaps new ways for helping children would be found.

The purpose of the referral was to devise a motor-development program for David and to evaluate his vision. At my first visit I wished to evaluate ocular motility, eye-hand coordination, form perception, and refractive state (far-sight, shortsight, or astigmatism). The principle that had been firmly established in my clinic was to make the evaluation activity meaningful for the child.

To evaluate his ocular motility, I set up an HO electric train on a circular track with a diameter of thirty-six inches. The eye-hand coordination would be a simple manual response to a visual situation—he would be asked to stop the train in the station by learning to operate the transformer. Form perception could be investigated by asking him to build a bridge for the train and a garage for the cars. Finger control could be estimated by constructing bridges with the Lincoln Junior Engineering Set, which makes use of large bolts and screws. I planned to scope his eyes (objective determination of the refraction) while he was following the train.

When David arrived, I was ready for him. On the floor of the training room I had the HO train running. The room was semidark, and the engine light cast an eerie glow on the track. David easily separated from his mother and joined me on the floor near the train. He soon learned to operate the train. He could stop the train in the station at will. He moved readily to the next activity —building a bridge over the track. He showed good form perception and he readily placed the blocks for the bridge in the same pattern I had constructed in advance (Figure 3). As anticipated, he had some difficulty with fine finger control in building the bridge with the engineering set. His ocular motility was unsteady; however, he could keep his eyes on the moving train by rotating his head. The scoping showed that he had alternating monocular vision. David learned to build a garage for a small fleet of cars. Although David rarely answered, I nevertheless kept up a steady stream of conversation directly related to the activities. David would prefer to nod, rather than answer. It was evident from his responses that he understood my language.

FIGURE 3. Form Reproduction

Building a bridge for a train—
meaningful form perception.

FIGURE 4. Tongue Tracing

Licking powdered sugar, tracing
the lines on the form—training
in form perception.

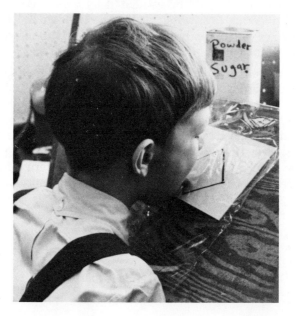

The first interview lasted for forty-five minutes; I was greatly encouraged by David's performance and comprehension. I scheduled three training periods per week, beginning with thirty-minute sessions, gradually increasing the time to one hour. The visual therapy was centered around the train, the cars, and the buildings. David moved the cars around the training room while on his hands and knees; this was the most meaningful way to integrate the arms and legs. At the beginning of the second month of training, David could draw the track (circle) and the garage (square). To teach David how to draw geometric forms, I showed him how to trace the forms on wax paper with his tongue. Under the wax paper I placed the shape to be learned, and then I dusted powdered sugar on the wax paper. David was told to trace the lines with his tongue, and he was rewarded by licking the "candy sugar," as he called it (Figure 4).

Six weeks after the beginning of David's training program, he was reevaluated by the psychologist. This was the first time that he could make any meaningful assessment of the boy. David was able to sit still and respond to the test directions. The psychologist's faith in the boy's intelligence was firmly justified; he was not retarded—it would be a long, uphill struggle, but there was hope.

David soon learned to speak; he discovered his parents and showed real affection for the first time. David attended school in a special class. He learned to read and write, but he still has some difficulties in arithmetic. He completed ten years of schooling and is presently receiving vocational training.

A Meaningful Perceptual-Motor Curriculum

1. Ocular motility.	HO train.
2. Eye-hand coordination.	Stopping the HO train in station and following the train on the track with flashlight in darkened room.
3. Form reproduction.	Building bridges and garages.
4. Finger dexterity.	Wooden hardware (bolts, screws, nuts, etc.).
5. Creeping (hands and knees).	Pushing toys and treasure hunt.
6. Form reproduction through tracing.	Tracing sugar-coated shapes with tongue.
7. Balancing activities.	Balance-beam games of crossing bridges, overpass for train.
8. Binocular vision.	Red Glass drawing (see Glossary), placing pickup stick in a straw.

THE STORY OF ALICE—THE GIRL WHO TALKED TOO MUCH

In my work with Alice, I became aware of the importance of body image in mental health. She was referred to our center for assessment and training by a psychologist in the child care section of the department of psychiatry of a large general hospital. Alice had been in therapy for four years. The psychological assessment showed that Alice, on the *Wechsler Intelligence Scale for Children*, had normal intelligence: Verbal Scale 114—Performance Scale 92. The psychiatric report indicated that she suffered from acute anxiety, with a rich fantasy life; she had no peer relationships and she was very hostile to her parents. Alice did not respond to play therapy nor would she enter into the social program at the hospital.

She was eleven years old, slender, with sallow complexion. Alice clung to her mother during the interview and talked incessantly. She spoke of her anxiety about doctors and asked me please not to cut her. Her incessant speech, which was often unrelated to the situation, was full of illusions of personal body harm. Alice was insecure in space; she would not cross the street alone and had to be taken to and from school by her mother. She did not participate in the classroom and was regarded by both teachers and pupils as "mental."

The visual-motor analysis showed that Alice had poor motor skills, both gross and fine; she was unable to complete a preschool form board without help, and she could not negotiate the four-inch walking rail.

Alice was accepted for four weeks of diagnostic training. During this period we hoped to learn more about her abilities as we tried to find procedures that were meaningful to her. We noticed that she would not enter the theatre where we do our darkroom projection training. She remained at the doorway, afraid to enter. The development of body image was our first major goal. It seemed that her inability to sense her body dimensions made her incapable of crossing the street—and contributed to her fear of mutilation. Her poor body image justified her fear of the street and unfamiliar places.

Body Image Development Program

The program that was designed for Alice consisted of vibrator stimulation of the skin surfaces. At first she was afraid of the hand vibrator; we let her hold it and she used it on the therapist until she would permit him to use it on her back and limbs. Log rolling (child rolls on the floor with hands placed by the sides) was used to give her back and front integration and to develop reciprocal innervation. Later she was taught to roll in the barrel. A large fibre detergent drum is used as a barrel. The bottom is removed so that the child can climb through. The child curls up in the barrel and makes it roll. It is important to keep the fingers inside the barrel and not in the edge or rim to avoid hurting the fingers. The activity provides body image training.

Alice also participated in obstacle course programs in which she had to fit her body through various sized openings. Her favorite game was limbo; this consisted of going between sticks that were gradually brought closer together. After three weeks she attempted the balance beam, and in six weeks she was jumping on the trampoline, which is used in accordance with the principle of the organizing role played by the visual sense. The transport and balance mechanisms of the body serve the telereceptors. In accordance with this principle, the children read charts while jumping in the trampoline. The Arrows chart (see Chapter 3) can serve for children who cannot read print. The children point in the direction of the arrows as they jump on the trampoline. In this way the balance mechanism serves vision. It is not an end in itself.

The change in her behavior was dramatic; her fantasies about body harm had diminished and she would now cross the street with another child—this indicated an improvement in peer relations as well as more security in space. In her therapy at the hospital she was able to participate in the social program, while in school she was willing to answer questions orally for the first time and she became concerned about her scholastic standing. Her incessant speech pattern was replaced by more appropriate speech. Alice used incessant speech in the same way that a cat uses her whiskers to negotiate space in the dark. When she could negotiate space visually, there was no further need for excessive speech.

The Program for Alice: General Skin Stimulation

After Alice became accustomed to the hand vibrator, our occupational therapist presented general skin stimulation in the following games:

Game 1 — Identification of Body Parts: The vibrator was held gently on the back of her head and she was asked, "What part am I touching? Now show me exactly where I touched your body." Thus she named the parts and located them by touch. By touching two or more parts, a memory factor was introduced.

Game 2 — Touch and Show: Alice was asked to bring her doll to the office. The therapist touched Alice and said, "Show me on the doll where I touched you." She was soon able to project her perception of body parts to the doll (Figure 5).

FIGURE 5. *Body Image Training*

The vibrator touches a part of the body.
The child must show the part touched
by pointing to the doll.

Game 3 — Treasure Hunt: The aim of this game was to improve locomotion. Rolling is the ideal training for the development of reciprocal innervation. Body movement is affected by opposing muscle systems (flexors-extensors). In order to achieve smooth movement, the stimulation to the flexors must be reduced while the neural flow to the extensors must be increased. Any disruption of this process results in one set of muscles "fighting" the opposing set. Alice had jerky movements and showed an inability of control and direct movement. Our first objective was to teach her to roll over. This required integration of the major muscle systems of the back and trunk through reciprocal innervation. Barrel rolling and treasure hunt gave her this much-needed experience. In treasure hunt, she could hunt for the objects by rolling to them—no other form of locomotion was allowed. Later, when the rolling became smooth, creeping and crawling were introduced.

Alice was diagnosed as being emotionally disturbed, and she had made slow progress in traditional psychotherapy. Her improvement taught us the value of body image training. But her story does not end here. In Chapter 3, she is part of the story of how our program of multisensory motor-training evolved.

REFERENCES

1. W. S. McCullogh, *Vision* (New York, N.Y.: Paul B. Hoeber, Inc., 1949), p. 4.

2. H. F. R. Prechtl, *Reading Disability* (Baltimore, Md.: The Johns Hopkins Press, 1962), p. 191.

Chapter 2. FUNDAMENTALS OF REMEDIATION

In this chapter you will find new techniques for children with space and language problems. The Kirshner Body Alphabet is a gross-motor approach to beginning reading. Sensorimotor integration, involving vision, hearing, directionality, speech, and movement is a new method of evaluating children. The child in total action demonstrating his level of achievement may well replace the more traditional measures of performance of our children. You will find games to improve motor skills—beginning with eye movements, and progressing to eye-hand coordination, binocular vision, and finger control.

How does a therapist help a child? He makes use of his training and he attempts to adapt it to the specific needs of the child. The translation of theory into practice is the art of teaching. This is the lonely road that every therapist must travel; when he faces the child there is no comfort in theory. His mentors are powerless, his past experience irrelevant—what counts is that he must make contact with this child NOW.

The remedial programs described in this book are the attempts to make contact in the NOW with the child. I cannot always get the same results with these procedures, nor have all my teachers been successful using these techniques—each teacher had to cross the lonely road and make contact in the NOW. If there has been any success in using these programs, it has been due to the intuition, warmth, creativity, and sensitivity of the teacher.

KIRSHNER BODY ALPHABET AND BODY IMAGE

Did you ever notice how hard it is to judge motion when you are looking at the station from a slowly moving train? Your knowledge of the world around you is reliable when you have a fixed point of reference. Before the child develops the fixed point of reference for judging his external world, he must first develop a fixed internal reference so that he knows where his arms, legs, and trunk are situated in relation to each other. According to leading authorities,[1] the information coming from the muscles, tendons, and balance mechanism (vestibular apparatus) must be collected and organized. This process of perceiving body parts and their relations is known as *body schema* or *body image*.

Children with learning disabilities show a high incidence of body image disorders.[2] The teacher is aware of this body image disorder when the child trips over the threshold and knocks over his books. The child is unaware of the space occupied by the extension of his arms and legs.

Authorities have found that imitation-of-movement games help in establishing a sound body image.[3] The Kirshner Body Alphabet (K.B.A.) is essentially an imitation-of-movement activity that comprises twenty-six postures, each one linked to a letter of the alphabet (Figure 6). The program follows the principles of child development by providing concrete kinesthetic experience prior to the more symbolic and abstract levels that are represented by form perception. Grace M. Fernald made a great contribution to special education when she introduced kinesthetic reinforcement into reading instruction.[4] The K.B.A. follows this tradition by introducing gross-motor reinforcement of letter symbols in preschool, primary, and special education.

When the child assumes the position of the letter, as shown in Figure 6, he is associating the feeling of body parts with the shape *and* the name of the letter. The kinesthetic feedback, stimulated by the positioning of the body, reinforces the association and the perception. He feels the shape as he bends, stands, and stretches. This basic interlocking of his own movements is then integrated at the kinesthetic level, and prepares the child for the transition into the symbolic and then abstract levels necessary for more accurate perception of space and form.

K.B.A.—PRESCHOOL AND KINDERGARTEN

Objective: To imitate the movement of a demonstrator (teacher) and transfer the skill to print, through intermediate steps of charts and puppets. The materials for teaching the body alphabet includes a set of 8x12 inch charts of each posture; a set of slides in color; a wooden moveable puppet and work books.

The children are arranged in a straight line facing the teacher. They cannot learn the K.B.A. while standing in a circle with the demonstrator in the center because print is only seen from one side. The teacher says, "Children, today we are going to learn the *x*, *y*, and *t*. Here is the *x*," and she makes the posture. "Here is the *x*," and the teacher points to the *x* on the chart. "Here is the *x*," and the teacher selects the *x* puppet. "Here is the *x*," and the teacher writes the *x* on the chalkboard. After each demonstration, the children say, "Here is the *x*," and they make the posture. The teacher circulates around the class, adjusting the postures without drawing attention to the children who are in difficulty.

"Now we shall learn the *y*. Here is the *y*," and the procedure is repeated through the sequence: demonstrator, chart, puppet, and chalkboard. The chalkboard is used in a novel way in this program. Instead of asking the children to write the letters that may invite failure, the teacher makes the letters and asks the children to erase them with the index finger, following the directions from top down and from left to right. This provides tactual reinforcement of the letter shape with a high degree of success. (Learning the letter *names* is incidental to the training in preschool programs. Do not test the children by asking them

FIGURE 6. The Kirshner Body Alphabet

to perform the letter by name alone; always point to the chart or puppet when referring to a letter.)

The K.B.A. should be presented in the following sequence of lessons:

Lesson 1   x-y-t

Lesson 2   c-l-n

Lesson 3   o-r-s

Lesson 4   e-i-j (note difference between *i* and *l*, *i* and *j*)

Lesson 5   k-m-z

Lesson 6   f-g-q

Lesson 7   p-u-w

Lesson 8   a-b-h (note difference between *b* and *h*)

Lesson 9   a-d-v (body balance is important for the letter *v*)

Suggested Schedule:

Preschool: 3 new letters every two weeks—total program 18 weeks.

Kindergarten: 3 new letters every week—total program 9 weeks.

Chalkboard Procedure

After the letters have been learned in each lesson, the teacher writes them on the board, and each child is given three letters to erase (three *x*'s, for example). The art lesson can be used to reinforce the letters, by coloring, cutting, and pasting activities.

Orientation

It is important that the correction of the children's postures should be non-verbal and gentle. If there is a directional problem, simply turn the child around—do not be concerned if the problem persists, the directional skills mature between the ages of five and six. The practice of K.B.A. is a fundamental part of the treatment of directional problems, since the child is taught a motor-kinesthetic pattern in relation to a visual form.

For letters that are symmetrical, such as *x-y-t*, the children face the teacher and perform the mirror image. All the other letters have a directional component and the children face the same *side* of the room as the demonstrator.

The sticks shown in Figure 6 are made by rolling a piece (12 x 36 inches) of red cardboard into a tube and securing it with scotch tape. This makes the 36-inch stick for the letter *a*. The long stick (for *d*, *h*, etc.) is made by stapling two pieces of cardboard with enough overlap to make a stick 60 inches in length. A long and short stick is provided for each child. Dowel sticks (5/8th inch in diameter), painted red, may also be used, but these might be dangerous and require a safety procedure.

Puppet Training

The puppets are directional; always present them with the front surface facing the child. They are useful for tactual reinforcement; the children can explore the letter shapes in three dimensions and thus add many new tactual and kinesthetic experiences to their sense repertoire—all related to reading.

Tactual Visualization

This skill may be developed by playing a blindfold game: the children must identify the puppet by touch and then make the Body Alphabet letter.

Relay Race

The group is divided into two teams. The puppets are also divided into two "teams" and placed across the room, opposite the children. The first two children run to the puppets, quickly make the body shape, pick up the puppet, and run back. When they return to the team, the next runner is touched and he runs across the room, makes the body shape of the next puppet, picks it up, and runs back to the next member of the team. This game should be played after the children have mastered all of the letter forms.

K.B.A.—GRADES ONE THROUGH FIVE

Children who are learning the Body Alphabet for the first time in grade one should be introduced to the letters in alphabetical sequence. The children should follow the lead of the demonstrator and transfer immediately to the chart. Whether the teacher chooses to use letter *names* is an individual matter. In many schools, the letter *sounds* are used for identification. Three letters per lesson can readily be mastered, and new letters should be introduced every two days. The suggestions for correcting errors given in the preschool and kindergarten should be followed. The lessons should be given in the following sequence:

GRADE 1:

Lesson 1   a-b-c

Lesson 2   d-e-f

Lesson 3   g-h-i

Lesson 4   j-k-l

Lesson 5   m-n-o

Lesson 6   p-q-r

Lesson 7   s-t-u

Lesson 8   v-w-x

Lesson 9   y-z

GRADE 2 — 6 letters per day.

GRADE 3 — 8 letters per day.

GRADE 4 — 12 letters per day.

GRADE 5 and up — all letters may be given in a single lesson.

TEACHING READING WITH K.B.A.

Directed Reading

After nine letters have been mastered, words may be introduced. The teacher asks for volunteers to make simple two-, three-, and four-letter words. The teacher says, "Please make the word *c-a-b*." Three volunteers go to the front of the room and decide who will make each letter and what space they will occupy. It is very important for the teacher to allow self-direction for this part of the activity, even though this may take more time. But the directed reading, the read-along-with-me technique, ensures that all children can read the words; thus, there are no reading failures. Chalkboard association is used at this point. After the children have performed the word, each one goes to the chalkboard and writes the letter that he has shaped.

Controlled Vocabulary

When all of the letters have been mastered, the teacher posts word lists from Basal Readers. The children may select any word from the list to perform in front of the class. Team response is encouraged. While everyone can see and hear the words, those children who might have failed if they were directed to read the word out loud are given another opportunity to learn. This reduces the anxiety in beginning reading.

Self-directed Reading

Divide the class into teams of three or four players. Each team has a conference to pick any word. In a class of thirty, there may be from seven to ten teams. It is possible to have two teams present their words simultaneously as long as there is a wide space between each word. The children who observe the team words may write these words or read them aloud. Once again, the chalkboard writing is completed after the Body Alphabet word has been made. Each child writes the letter that he has shaped.

Gymnasium Program

The gym teacher can play a variety of games with K.B.A.

Game 1—Freeze: This game is played when the instructor blows his whistle and calls a letter. (This is a quick-paced game; do not form letters that require sticks.) "Who can be the first one to make the shape?" By increasing the number of letters, there is an opportunity to increase the memory span. The letters should be random and not in word form; for example, the teacher blows his whistle and calls "x-p-q-r," and the children perform this sequence. He may then ask one pupil to make the sequence while the rest of the class determines if it is right or wrong.

Game 2—Send a Message: The group is divided into four teams—six or seven players per team. The north and south teams send messages (communicate via the Body Alphabet) to each other across the gym while the east and west teams do the same. Three sets of sticks are given to each team. For children in primary grades who play this game, word lists may be prepared by the teacher, with one word list posted near each team. But it is useful to allow the teams self-direction. The instructor is a resource person who may be called upon to help members who have forgotten a letter form.

Game 3—Make a Message: The format is the same as Game 2, except that the pupils are free to choose their own words.

Game 4—Long Distance: The instructor should encourage the use of K.B.A. for communication games in the schoolyard or in the hallways. On field trips, use binoculars for helping the pupils to relay information over a long distance.

K.B.A. for Scouting

Communication is one of the cornerstones of the scouting movement. Semaphore flags and the Morse code are standard methods of communication. The Kirshner Body Alphabet makes a good backup communication system when the traditional systems cannot be used. It takes one year of practice in the Morse code before the operator can receive and transmit twelve words per minute, and unless there is consistent practice, the system is lost. It takes several hours of intensive practice or several months of spaced practice with semaphore flags before they can be used, and this system of letter symbols also must be practiced frequently. K.B.A. has been taught to a grade four class, average age ten, in twenty-five minutes, after which the children were able to transmit and receive messages, either by the whole-word method or by serial exposure, in which one person makes each letter in the proper sequence.

K.B.A. VISUALIZATION

Visualization is the ability to manipulate past experience without sensory input. Thus, it is possible to visualize a lion without having the animal in view. The ability to visualize is the heart of symbolic learning, planning, and efficient behavior. The phrase "back to the drawing board" represents a failure in visualization. The visualization function is an inherent part of the K.B.A. system. In order to perform the Body Alphabet, two skills are required: (1) body image, to establish the correct relationship between the limbs, the trunk, and gravity; and (2) visualization.

Even though the person performing the K.B.A. cannot see his whole posture, he must operate as if he were also the observer so that he can determine whether or not the direction of the letter is appropriate for the reader (observer). Thus, he must visualize what the observer is seeing. Many adults reverse the letters *e*, *s*, and *z* when they perform the K.B.A. because they fail to visualize the appearance of their body to the "external" observer. To gain practice in visualization for advanced training, the pupil should be able to perform between two groups of observers. (See Figure 7 for the relationships.) The teacher

FIGURE 7. Training in Visualization

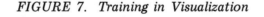

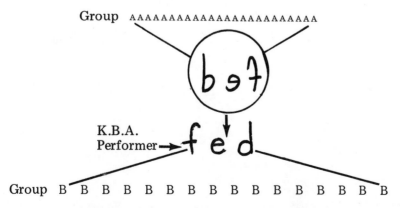

The word *f-e-d* observed by Group B is seen reversed by Group A. The performer is asked to make some words that can be seen in proper orientation by Group A or B. For example, he makes the words "See me" for Group B and "Bad boy" for Group A. The performer must try to imagine how each group is seeing him—this is visualization. Note: the person performing the body alphabet is situated between the two groups.

can ask the pupil to make the first word for group A and the second word for group B. When he is performing for group B, he must orient his body 180 degrees from the position he used when he performed his letters for group A.

REFERENCES

1. A. Jean Ayres, "Patterns of Perceptual Motor Dysfunction in Children," *Perceptual and Motor Skills*, 20 (1965); Ray Barsch, *Achieving Perceptual Motor Efficiency* (Seattle, Wash.: Special Child Publications, Inc., 1967); M. Frostig, D. W. Lefever, J. R. B. Whittlesey, *Developmental Test of Visual Perception* (Palo Alto, Calif.: Consulting Psychologists Press, 1964); G. N. Getman, *How to Develop Your Child's Intelligence* (Luverne, Minn.: Research Publications, 1965); Sir Henry Head, *Studies in Neurology* (London: Oxford University Press, 1920).

2. Myrene McAninch, "Body Image as Related to Perceptual-Cognitive Motor Disabilities," *Learning Disorders*, ed. Jerome Helmuth (Seattle, Wash.: Special Child Publications, Inc., 1966).

3. Barsch, *Achieving Perceptual Motor Efficiency*; Getman, *How to Develop Your Child's Intelligence*; N. C. Kephart, *The Slow Learner in the Classroom* (Columbus, Ohio: Charles E. Merrill Books, Inc., 1960).

4. Grace M. Fernald, *Remedial Techniques in Basic School Subjects* (New York, N.Y.: McGraw-Hill Book Company, 1943).

Chapter 3. INTEGRATION

The human being is a SEEINGHEARINGREMEMBERINGSPEAKINGMOVING organism. Attempts to know the human being by "measuring" fragmented aspects of his performance in Information, Vocabulary, Arithmetic, Picture Arrangement, etc., often conceal more than they reveal. This chapter discusses a new thrust in the measurement of human performance.

Alice (see Chapter 1) had great difficulty accepting sensory stimulation. She reacted negatively to sights and sounds. For example, bright lights bothered her. When she visited the supermarket with her mother, she became confused. The colors, lights, and movements were more than she could tolerate. Loud noises would disturb her; she would often cover her ears when other children were noisy. It soon became apparent that we would have to gradually introduce multiple sensory stimulation as she became proficient in each modality. This problem lead to the development of the multisensory motor-training program described in this chapter.

Our experience with Alice shows that sensorimotor integration plays a strong role in the mental health and emotional development of the child. A rehabilitation program must focus not only on the psychodynamics of the child for emotional development, peer relations, and family relations through the traditional approaches of the psychotherapist, but it must also reduce the real anxiety which is related to the child's inability to handle sensory information or to adequately perform the skilled acts required for day-to-day living. A new member of the therapeutic team must therefore be the sensorimotor specialist.

SEEINGHEARINGREMEMBERINGSPEAKINGMOVING

Marshall McLuhan provided us with powerful insights on the effect of media on perception.[1] The tribal world of preliterate man made use of a harmonious integrated sensorium. The world of the Gutenberg print technology isolated the visual sense from the sensorium, and set the stage for the learning-disabled child.

In order to understand the effect of print on man's visual sense, it is first necessary to understand the role of vision in nature. According to Sir W. Stewart Duke-Elder, sight was designed to guide and direct movement.[2] When the capacity to guide movement is lost, the organism faces extinction. Many children who enter school manifest visual disabilities. An anthropological definition of a visual disability is that the visual sense has lost its relationship to the whole sensorium, the tactual, the kinesthetic, and the auditory. Reading depends upon form perception of letter shapes integrated with letter sounds. The alienation of the sense of sight frustrates the student's ability to read.

Let us consider the development of vision in the preschool years. A. Gesell and his coworkers have systematically catalogued the infant's awakening to the world of light.[3] Objects in space have no meaning until he has reached out and touched, and tasted, and manipulated the objects around him. He begins to cement and bind the visual data to the touch, smell, texture, and resistance of the things he discovers. Later, if his lesson is well learned, he will see the "apple" and immediately bring to mind the taste, the flavor, the total experience. It is this capacity to see and know that helps him to master his world.

When the child is confronted with print for the first time, he experiences neither color, nor familiar form, nor surface, nor smell, nor thing. The configuration of the word *apple* does not have any apple in it. There is only a procession of strange shapes on a smooth ground. For the first time in his short life his past experience in the illuminated world is of no value to him. The visual sense now must grapple with forms and shapes that have no taste, texture, resistance, gravity, or "thingness." He would have to undergo a transformation before these strange shapes on a smooth ground would once more conjure up the apple. At this point he leaves the tribal world with its harmonious sensorium, where everything visual was also tactual, and he places a great burden on the visual sense—the burden of sanity and meaning. Preliterate man could read signs in the forest because a footprint, a bent twig, and a faint movement might herald the presence of a deadly enemy. The signs he read had depth and texture and cast a shadow, and when he touched them the eye and hand agreed. Clinical experience and research in perceptual-motor therapy clearly show that in order to make a literate eye one has to have a tribal eye.

Developing the Tribal Eye

Training the senses, extending their range and interweaving them is the curriculum. With love and patience, Maria Montessori helped her children put their world together by interweaving the sense of touch, movement, hearing, and seeing in meaningful activities—then and only then could the children rely on their vision.

A. M. Skeffington, G. N. Getman and others in the Optometric Extension Program provided us with a model of visual development that has helped children adapt to the world of print and electronic media. The concept of the four circles proposes the model from which curricula may be developed (Figure 8). Each circle represents an important subsystem to vision.

A. Antigravity—coming to terms with gravity in order to move.

B. Centering—the ability to locate objects in space.

C. Identification—the ability to store information.

D. Speech-Audition—the ability to communicate through language and gesture.

E.   The emergent process that comes from the interweaving of all of these modalities is vision.

FIGURE 8. *The Visual Processes*

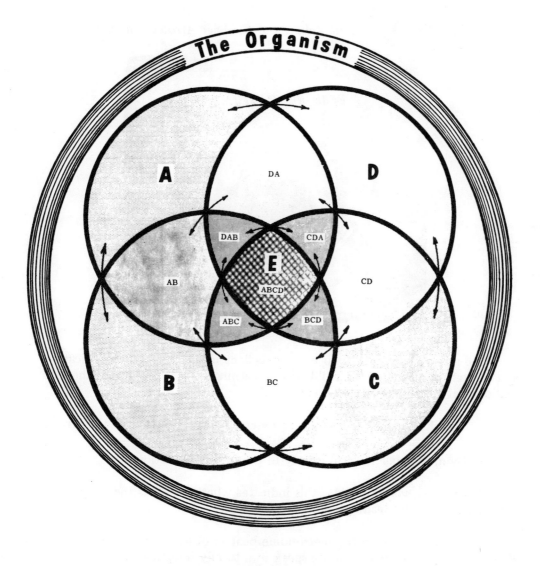

A: THE ANTIGRAVITY PROCESS
B: THE CENTERING PROCESS
C: THE IDENTIFICATION PROCESS
D: THE SPEECH-AUDITION PROCESS
E: THE EMERGENT: VISION

I have devised many training procedures that come from this model. The first of these games was the Kirshner Arrows, in which the objective is to integrate sight, audition, movement, and speech.

Putting the Child Together

The Kirshner Arrows chart provides a training procedure that grows directly out of the concept of the four circles. The children point in the direction of the arrows while they name the side: right, left, up, down (Figure 9). The rhythm is supplied by a metronome set at 60.

FIGURE 9. Student Taking the Kirshner Arrows Training

The arrows have proved to be an excellent means of both identification and the rehabilitation of the child with a learning disorder. Consider the information that they provide to the examiner.

1. The child must use his *eyes* to determine the direction of the arrows.

2. He must *move* his arm crisply in the desired direction.

3. He must *name* the side—this indicates whether he has the proprioceptive awareness of his leading side.

4. He must *listen* to the metronome beat in order to trigger his responses. When the child can hear-see-move-speak in a totally integrated manner, he is ready to face the world of concepts and print.

If the child cannot perform the arrows test, we gradually reduce the demand. First we remove the need to identify right and left. If the child still cannot perform the task, we reduce the demand once more by removing the need to speak. If the child still cannot keep the rhythm and point in the direction indicated by the arrows, we once again drop the demand by removing the arrows and asking him to keep time to the metronome. As soon as the child's level of integration has been determined, we gradually increase the demands until he is fully organized. Preliminary testing of kindergarten children with the arrows shows that it is more closely related to achievement than intelligence tests.[4]

Visual Folk Dance

The idea of the Visual Folk Dance came to me while I was visiting the Centre for Culture and Technology at the University of Toronto. While I was demonstrating the total integration of the sensorium to Marshall McLuhan and Harley Parker, by means of the Arrows, it occurred to me with great force that the program lacked esthetic value. I had been too conscious of the sensorimotor mechanisms and not enough thought was devoted to the total meaning of the behavior. The directors of the Center approved wholeheartedly my decision to rethink the movement patterns and substitute a more pleasing performance.

I designed dance figures in Elizabethan costumes (Figure 10), set them up in a sequence of total body movement patterns, and added music in place of the metronome. On my next visit to the Centre for Culture and Technology, I presented the Visual Folk Dance to the students and associates. The Elizabethan figures were arranged in a smooth sequence of integrated movements and the music was supplied by a virtuoso banjo player. It was fun to watch a group of adults experiencing vision, audition, and kinesthesia united in the classical mode of the dance.

FIGURE 10. *Visual Folk Dance*

Children copy the figures
to the rhythm of music.

Developing Fine-Motor Skills

In order to develop the readiness for writing it is important for the fingers to be flexible and supple. Many children have failed to develop the thumb and finger opposition. In order to assist in this development, the Fingers chart is used (Figure 11). The child looks at the chart and makes the finger patterns that he sees; with practice he will begin to develop the thumb-finger opposition that is necessary to perform these patterns. Once he is able to hold up any number of fingers desired, we use the program to integrate vision, hearing, movement, and speech. We ask the child to tell how many fingers he makes in each pattern to the beat of the metronome set at 60. Once again as with the arrows, if the total integration is not possible, we gradually drop the demands one at a time until we have found the point where the child can achieve. For example, for some children it may be necessary to remove the metronome. As the visual efficiency and manual dexterity gradually increase, it will be possible to reintroduce the auditory factor.

FIGURE 11. *Student Taking Fine-motor Training with the Fingers Chart*

Testing Children

It has been the custom of child-care specialists to evaluate children by isolating one factor at a time and measuring it. Thus, while the child is seated he is tested for Information on one of the WISC subtests; there is nothing else demanded of him but this one element. Later, his performance in making visual judgments is tested in the Block Assembly subtest. Again, this one ability is isolated; for example, the auditory factor is not included.

In the early days of research in human behavior it may have been profitable to work in this controlled, single-factor methodology. Now the time has come to deal in more dynamic terms. Although it may be shown that a child has information when he takes a psychological test, does he have it when he needs it? Can the child respond quickly to his teacher's question during classroom discussions? Does he have information in discussing current events with his family or friends? Although he may have a good score on visual perception on a standardized test, can he detect the best position for a pass in basketball, can he keep track of a rapidly shifting field and make a decision in a fraction of a second as to where the ball should be passed? One of the most impressive illustrations of sensorimotor readiness is the Australian aborigine child who can detect the movement of a mouse in a gray stoney field at a distance of 100 feet and pick up a small stone and strike this animal within a matter of a few seconds. I often wonder if the exquisite art of the Eskimos, the smooth flowing lines and loving attention to details, is not in some way related to their freedom of movement over the ice and snow as they pit their forces against the inhospitable environment.

In order to prepare our children for survival in the modern urban environment, we may have to build the perceptual-motor freedom of the tribal worlds of the bushman, aborigine, and Eskimo. This will allow the vision to soar to new heights of freedom and bring with it the richness of the world of things, feelings, and movement.

TRAINING FOR THE BRIGHT BOY
WHO COULD NOT GET PROMOTED

Problem:

Jimmy (see Chapter 1) could not keep his place while reading.

Training:

Eye movement training

 —following the Marsden Ball and shooting it with a rubber-tipped dart.

 —rotating movies.

 —quick fixations using two projectors.

Problem:

Jimmy could not write quickly and neatly.

Training:

Ball bouncing routines.

Chalkboard circles.

Problem:

Jimmy could not concentrate while reading.

Training:

Optometric visual training. Jimmy suppressed his eyes periodically and had faulty muscle balance. Lenses to improve ocular balance were prescribed, and fusion drawing was used to keep the two eyes working at all times. How did these problems contribute to Jimmy's reading difficulty? Consider what was happening when Jimmy suppressed the vision in one eye and the two eyes were not pointing to the same word because of his faulty muscle balance. While his right eye was reading, he could follow the story line; however, when his left eye switched off (suppression), he was no longer looking at the same word. The continuity was broken and Jimmy lost patience. Jimmy made rapid progress because visual training was used in conjunction with motor training. This shows clearly that children who require remedial reading should be screened and trained by an optometrist or ophthalmologist who provides this wide range of professional service. Through the postgraduate training provided by the Optometric Extension Program, more than 4,000 optometrists are providing this form of training.

Problem:

Jimmy did not have a high motivation for reading.

Training:

Model building and radio construction that required the reading of plans.

Plus lenses were provided for Jimmy when the visual training was started. He wore them at all times in the classroom and for study at home. Since he had 20/20 vision, they were not designed to make his seeing clearer or larger. They were prescribed to make his seeing and learning easier; not as a sign of a defect, not as a "tool" for his job of learning. The lenses alone, without the visual training, would not have made the marked changes in his achievement, and vice versa. But together, they let him make tremendous improvements.

TRAINING GAMES TO IMPROVE LEARNING

The sequence of training followed in this book is based on A. Gesell and Jean Piaget. According to Piaget, sensorimotor intelligence precedes cognitive intelligence.[5] The Gesell scale was discussed on page 18. For convenience it is included here because it is applicable to the general purpose of the training mentioned in this chapter: the child's path of motor development during the first year:

4 weeks	Ocular Control
16 weeks	Head Balance
28 weeks	Hand Grasp and Manipulation (eye-hand coordination)
40 weeks	Finger Control

Eye-Movement Control

According to David Robinson, professor of biomedical engineering, Johns Hopkins Medical School, the eye has four systems of control. The first system helps us see an object clearly; the image must be focused on a very small area of the eye known as the fovea. When an object is moving, the eye muscles must produce smooth movement in order to keep the image on the vital area. Games that develop *smooth eye control* will be described.

In order to quickly locate an object, the eyes must possess a quick and accurate aiming mechanism. When the child reads to the end of the line, his eyes must jump quickly and accurately to the beginning of the next line. Games to develop *quick fixations* are next.

Even when the head and body are moving, the eyes must be able to maintain contact with a moving target. To accomplish this, the eye-movement mechanism must be linked directly to the position of the head and trunk. When a gun is fired from a moving battleship, there is a mechanism that compensates for the pitch and roll of the ship; thus, it maintains its aim under all conditions. *Developing body balance skills while viewing a fixed or moving target* helps to develop this mechanism in children.

The fourth mechanism required for eye-movement control keeps both eyes on the target regardless of the distance from the eyes. The range finder on a battleship is comprised of two telescopes which are placed apart from each other on the ship at a prescribed distance. The amount of convergence of the two telescopes as they are aligned with the target helps to determine its distance from the ship. In children, training the two eyes to look from near to far helps to develop this *binocular alignment skill*. The four mechanisms are:

1. Smooth tracking.
2. Quick fixations.
3. Compensation for body movement.
4. Binocular alignment.

Developing Smooth Control of the Eyes

Game 1—Marsden Ball: This device was developed by Carl D. Marsden, an optometrist from Colorado. It consists of a sponge ball suspended from the ceiling by a string. Letters and forms are pasted on the ball. Children are asked to read the letters as the ball swings. In the first position, the child lies on his back while he views the ball swinging in a circle. Later, he follows the same procedure from a standing or sitting position.

Game 2—Shoot the Ball: To maintain interest in the activity, use a rubber-tipped dart gun or bow and arrow and ask the child to shoot the swinging ball.

Game 3—Guess the Card: Two children play this game. One child holds a playing card, picture card, letter of the alphabet, or dice in his hand with his arm extended (Figure 12). He rotates the arm slowly while he presents the *back of the card* to his partner. While the card is rotating at the rate of one complete circle every two seconds, he turns the card around so that his partner can name it. For preschool or kindergarten children, use picture cards.

FIGURE 12. *Eye-Movement Training*

Guess-the-card game. Card is moved in a circle and child must name it.

Game 4—Arithmetic or Spelling Game: To play arithmetic the child must add the number of cards as they are successively presented in the above game. (Do not go beyond his arithmetic range.) For the spelling game use three or four letters and ask him to compose a word. The dice can be used in place of the numbered cards.

Kirshner Oculo-Rotor Training: This training utilizes an instrument that was designed to provide group training for children with learning difficulties. It has a variety of applications and is especially useful for eye-movement training. The

Oculo-Rotor, a device that consists of a revolving mirror that can be varied in rotation rate, is used in conjunction with a slide or movie projector (Figure 13). The picture is reflected from the mirror onto a large screen or a blank wall surface. The child follows the target (picture) with his eyes as it revolves. This instrument measures eye-movement skill by determining the fastest rotation rate at which the child can see a target that requires 50 percent (20/40) vision. Studies show that by the age of six the eye can view the target at 40 rpm through an angle of 21 degrees. A target that rotates through a diameter of four feet when viewed from a distance of ten feet is seen from an angle of 21 degrees.

FIGURE 13. *Kirshner Oculo-Rotor*

A variable speed rotating mirror that produces rotating movies or slides.

High interest targets should be projected onto the revolving mirror. Movies, slides, and SVE (Society for Visual Education) lessons may be employed. The combined use of a projector and the Oculo-Rotor provides training in smooth, continuous eye rotations. The pictures may also be projected on the ceiling—the child should be in a supine position on the floor. In this case, the instrument should be set at 20 rpm and the direction is changed every sixty seconds.

Quick Fixation Training

The value of quick fixation training for the child is that it improves his accuracy in reading, particularly for moving his eyes from the end of the line over a long distance to the beginning of the next line. Two interesting visual targets are required for this training. They should be placed in the room about ten feet apart and ten feet from the child. This kind of training can be provided by using two projectors, each one pointing to a different part of the room. The picture should be changed while the child looks from one picture to the other. In order to project one picture at a time, the teacher covers one projector lens with a card while the other one is showing its picture, then she quickly moves the card to cover the other projector lens. Two film strip projectors or two View-Master projectors may be used. The View-Master projectors have the advantage in that they are inexpensive and there is a wide variety of interesting material for projection.

The Kirshner Oculo-Rotor may also be used for quick fixation training. It has been designed to alternately change the illumination of the projectors from one flash every three seconds to one flash per one-half second. In order to provide a wide range of interesting targets, the View-Master projectors are used with the Ocular-Rotor. Two Deluxe 100 Watt No. 2446 or two Standard 30 Watt No. 2430 models can serve very effectively. The distance between targets is ten feet and the viewing distance is ten feet so that the angle is approximately 60 degrees. This provides ample range for saccadic movements. The movements can be in the horizontal, vertical, or diagonal planes.

Quick fixation training may be accomplished without these special instruments. *Find the Number* is a game that requires only a large chalkboard or wall space (Figure 14). This game combines eye movements with training in left and right. Numbers or letters are placed on two sides of the wall or chalkboard with a large space in between. The children find the number or letter and tell which side it is on. The teacher calls a number, the children search, point, and say whether it is on the left or right side. In order to ensure the efficient learning of directions, the numbers should be placed on other walls in the classroom: the front wall for one session, the side wall for the second session, and the rear wall for the third session.

FIGURE 14. *Find the Number*

Numbers may be made on chalkboard or placed on cards and attached to wall. They should be rearranged from time to time.

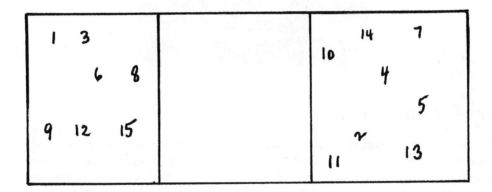

Eye Movements and Body Balance

In order to train the compensatory balance mechanisms related to the eye muscles, all the training described above can be combined with various gross-motor activities.

Rocking Board

Use one-half-inch plywood, ten by forty inches. Paint the upper surface red or yellow and add fine sand to the paint to create a nonslip surface. The child rocks from side to side as he follows the moving targets (Figure 15). For variations use the walking rail, the jumpboard, the trampoline, or have the children stand on one foot while they perform their visual tasks.

FIGURE 15. Eye Movements and Body Balance

Combining the eye movements with balance
activity. Child must rock on the board
while following the card.

Two-Eye Coordination

Aligning the two eyes on the one target is a very important requirement in
judging distance. In order to protect the individual from harm, the eyes have a
safety mechanism when alignment cannot be maintained; one eye suppresses its
image, thus preventing the appearance of double vision. Double vision creates a
danger because the individual cannot tell which is the true image. Negotiating
traffic with double vision is extremely hazardous.

The presence of suppression is an indication of imbalance in the ocular system. It may be created by unequal refractive conditions, low convergence re-
serve, and faulty focusing. An optometrist or ophthalmologist who has specialized in the rehabilitation of vision for learning should be consulted.

The Brock String may be used to detect the suppression. Use a twenty-
two inch white shoe lace and string a red bead on the lace. Measure four inches
from one end of the lace and make a black mark on it. Place one end of the
string on the forehead and be sure that the hand holding it does not block the
vision. Place the red bead at the end of the string farthest from the person and
ask him to look at the bead and tell which picture the string and bead resemble
(Figure 16). Next move the bead to the four-inch mark and ask the person to
look carefully at the red bead. Once again ask him which picture it resembles.

FIGURE 16. *Brock String Test*

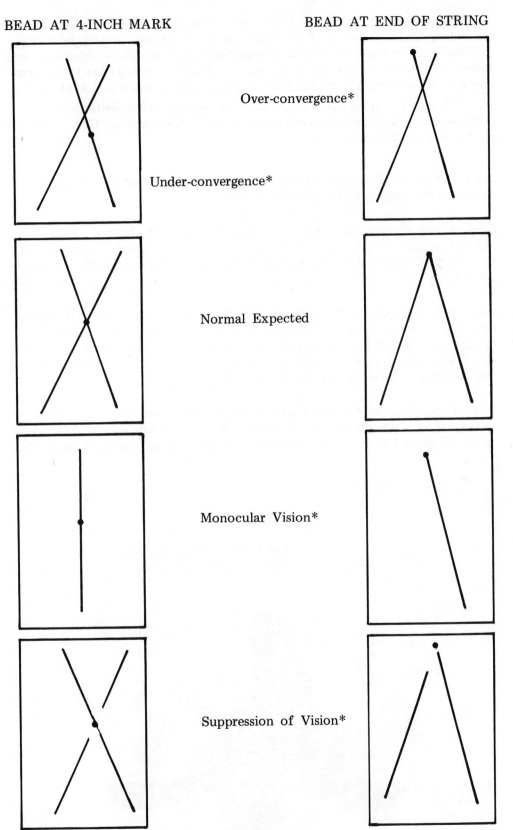

BEAD AT 4-INCH MARK   BEAD AT END OF STRING

Over-convergence*

Under-convergence*

Normal Expected

Monocular Vision*

Suppression of Vision*

*Shows abnormal function. Refer to specialist.

Eye-Hand Coordination

Jean Piaget, Jerome Bruner, A. Gesell and others have been very interested in the linking of hand and eye.[6] This process is not innate; it must be learned. Children who do not have sufficient opportunity to manipulate objects in their environment may develop lags in maturation. Rene Spitz describes the deterioration of children who were not given opportunities to move and explore space.[7]

Ball play is one of the best agents of eye-hand development. Teaching your child how to play ball opens doors to social development. How can we begin the ball skills with success?

Stage 1—Balloon: Using a balloon sets the stage for achievement. Play games that keep the balloon in the air. Age 3 to 5.

Stage 2—Ball Rolling: Have the child sit on the floor with his feet apart. Roll the ball to him and ask him to roll it back to you. The speed of the ball can be controlled; this enables him to match his arm extension with the visual target (Figure 17).

Stage 3—Ball Dropping: The ball is held in front of the body above the forehead. On the signal "Begin," he drops and catches the ball with both hands (Figure 18). Do not begin with ball bouncing; this may be too difficult a stage and it may set the pattern for failure. With practice the speed of ball dropping increases and it naturally leads to the next stage.

Stage 4—Ball Bouncing: Success can be assured if you ask the child to bounce the ball three times (Figure 19). Increase gradually until he can bounce indefinitely. When he has mastered bouncing with the preferred hand, begin the next stage.

FIGURE 17. Ball Rolling

Eye-hand coordination without fear of failure. Age 4 to 5.

FIGURE 18. *Ball Dropping*

The beginning of ball bouncing.
Age 4 to 5.

FIGURE 19. *Ball Bouncing*

Hit the X while bouncing ball.
Age 7.

Stage 5—Ball Bouncing (right-left, both, alternating): Once the skill of bouncing is established, link it with counting. This makes it a cognitive style of activity and helps to build the attention span and arithmetic concept. It is now possible to introduce refinements in ball bouncing. Teach him to avoid slapping the ball. More control can be acquired by bouncing the ball with a pushing motion than by slapping it. Diversify the activity: teach the use of the nonpreferred hand, then both hands together, and then alternating. As soon as alternating movements are introduced, you are beginning formal training in *motor planning*. The change in hand must be preplanned in order to meet the time demand. Motor planning has been linked with success in sports.

Stage 6—Ball Bouncing with Changing Posture: Bouncing while walking, running, sitting, hopping, and kneeling adds a strong body image factor to the training.

Stage 7—Bouncing Two Balls: Scandinavian physical education programs make extensive use of the ball. Bouncing two balls involves a new approach to bilateral planning. It is common for the beginner to lose control of the right hand (preferred hand) because when he makes the effort to increase the bounce of the nonpreferred hand, he cannot inhibit the impulse from his preferred side. Bouncing two balls helps to integrate the two halves of the body (Figure 20). It is easier to bounce both balls together in the same direction than in opposing directions. Once this first stage is mastered, introduce the alternate movements. To begin the bounce, raise one ball over the head and bring the hand down while the other hand is moving up; this helps to set up the alternating movements.

Stage 8—Body Bounce: Body bounce is extremely difficult; it calls for good body image and motor planning. Draw a chalkmark on the floor; it is important to bounce the ball on the mark at all times. Sit beside the floor mark with feet together so that the right knee is beside the mark. With the right arm extended, bounce the ball five times. After the fifth bounce, smartly move the right foot so that the mark is between the feet. Continue bouncing the ball five times in this new position. After the fifth bounce, move the left leg smartly so that the legs are touching once more and the mark is beside the left knee. Change to the left hand as the feet come together and bounce the ball with the left hand five times. Gradually reduce the number of bounces until there is one bounce in each position (Figure 21). The body bounce was demonstrated by professor Brian Cleary of McGill University.

FIGURE 20. Bouncing Two Balls

Age 8.

FIGURE 21. Body Bounce

Child bounces ball on his right, center, and left in sequence. Age 9.

Stage 9—Ball Bouncing and Visualization: Repeat all of the eight stages with the eyes closed. This calls for visualization. It is important to have a smooth floor and a high quality ball for this process.

Equipment: Seven-inch playground ball of Spalding or Voit quality is recommended. Gradually reduce the size of the ball as the skill develops until it can be accomplished with a La Crosse ball or a tennis ball.

Lesson Length: For the beginner, five minutes is sufficient time for a lesson. Do not increase the time to the point where fatigue begins to destroy the gains.

REFERENCES

1. Marshall McLuhan, *The Gutenberg Galaxy* (Toronto: University of Toronto Press, 1962); idem, *Understanding Media, The Extensions of Man* (New York, N.Y.: McGraw-Hill Book Company, 1964).

2. Sir W. Stewart Duke-Elder, *Textbook of Ophthalmology*, Vol. 1, 8th ed. (Philadelphia, Pa.: W. B. Saunders Company, 1960).

3. A. Gesell, *Vision: Its Development in Infant and Child* (New York, N.Y.: Paul B. Hoeber, Inc., 1949).

4. S. A. Dudek, A. J. Kirshner, and E. P. Lester, *Maturational Deficits and Learning in the Young Child*. Unpublished research in progress at McGill University, Montreal. This research is supported by Quebec Mental Health Grant 604-5-126. (See Appendix in this volume.)

5. Jean Piaget, *The Origins of Intelligence in Children* (New York, N.Y.: International Universities Press, Inc., 1952).

6. Piaget, *Origins of Intelligence*; Jerome Bruner, *Eye, Hand and Mind: Studies in Cognitive Development* (London: Oxford University Press, 1969); Gesell, *Vision*.

7. Rene Spitz, *The First Year of Life* (New York, N.Y.: International Universities Press, Inc., 1965), p. 53.

Chapter 4. LEARNING DISABILITY OR LAZY LEARNER?

In this chapter you will find a new space game—The Flying Tigers—that teaches children how to draw. You will learn how to distinguish between the Learning Disabled and the Lazy Learner.

How can you train a child who is so retarded that he cannot be measured on a formal test? How can you train a child who is so withdrawn that his attention cannot be sustained for more than a few seconds? In his monograph, *Eye, Hand and Mind*,[1] Jerome Bruner explores the early sensorimotor development of the child and finds that the eye-hand-mouth sequence is the fountainhead of the ability to perceive object relations. You will learn of the Rotating Lazy Susan technique, which can be employed with children at the lowest scale of development.

THE STORY OF SPACE AND LEARNING

How can you tell the difference between the Learning Disabled and the Lazy Learner? Make the drawings in Figure 22 and find out. Difficulty in making these drawings is an indication of a visual-perceptual weakness that may affect some aspects of learning. The basic difference between the lazy learner and the disabled learner is that *the lazy learner can and won't* and *the disabled learner can't in spite of normal intelligence*. It would be more accurate to say that he can't work at his intelligence level in school and is often two or three years below his potential in some areas.

FIGURE 22. Three Drawings for Copying Exercise in Visual Perception

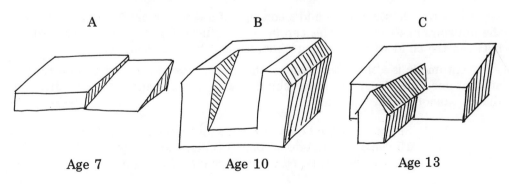

A B C

Age 7 Age 10 Age 13

What is Perception and How is It Related to Learning?

Perception is the meaning that comes from putting information together. How well we put together visual information can be shown by the drawings. Naturally, only one line can be drawn at a time. So, in order to make a good drawing, all the lines have to be put into the correct relationship. A child with a visual-perceptual disability cannot see the relationship between the lines; thus, he has trouble putting them together, as can be seen in the child's attempt to make Drawing A (Figure 23).

FIGURE 23. Child's Reproduction of Drawing A

Perceptual disability—student could
not show the third dimension.

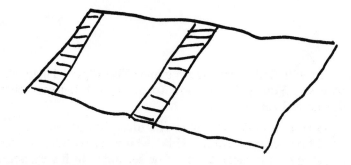

The child fails in this task because his "blanket is too short." When a tall person uses a short blanket and tries to cover his head, his feet stick out. A person with a perceptual disorder has trouble attending to more than two things at the same time. When he looks at a three-part picture and tries to remember it, it is just as though his "visual blanket" were too short; he always leaves one thing out.

Arithmetic Means Space

The child with a space problem can be handicapped in mathematics. Consider this question: "In what way is 15 related to 14 and 16?" The correct answer, "15 comes before 16 and after 14," requires an understanding of space. Here's another arithmetic problem: "Add 15.3 and 11." The child's answer depends upon his ability with space:

$$
\begin{array}{ccc}
15.3 & 15.3 & 15.3 \\
1\,1 & 11 & 11.0 \\
\hline
15.4 & 15.41 & 26.3
\end{array}
$$

How can we study the child's concept of space? By asking him to copy the drawings in Figure 22. This can help the educator and parent distinguish between the child with a learning disability and the lazy learner.

Arithmetic is a skill that requires the child to keep track of several things at the same time. There are many children who can add and subtract but nevertheless cannot do this example:

Suppose a pencil costs 10 cents and a tablet costs
15 cents and an eraser costs 8 cents, and you give
the man 50 cents. How much change do you get?

Teaching a child to see connections in space by drawing helps him to see connections in arithmetic. Of course, drawing ability, or space organization is only one of the skills necessary to do arithmetic. But when you consider that no one knows all the factors for success in mathematics, knowing space is a pretty good start.

The three drawings make a pretty good test of visual perception because at least half of the children of the same age in the neighborhood can do them. How do I know that so many kids in the neighborhood can do them? The story of these drawings began more than twenty years ago. A curriculum designer of the Montreal Protestant Schools thought it would be a good idea if students in grade nine could make complex freehand drawings. He reasoned that students must be able to make sketches and diagrams for biology, chemistry, physics, and science; thus, they should receive some training in sketching. Apparently most of the students could do them, so the drawings were retained in the high school curriculum. Suppose he had said, "I want everyone in the class to draw portraits." Most of these students would have flunked drawing. So portrait sketching is not a good test.

It seemed to me that if a fourteen-year-old student is expected to make these drawings, then the ability must develop gradually as he progresses from grade to grade. In order to find out when the skill developed, I asked Mrs. Audrey Deville, an education officer of the Chateauguay school board for help. She arranged for me to test sixty children in each grade from age six to fourteen. I soon had the answer. Seven-year-olds could draw the first picture (A), but they could not draw the second and third (B and C). A few eight-year-olds could draw the second picture but most of the children who could draw the second picture were ten years old. A few could draw the third picture, but it was not until age thirteen that most could draw the third picture.

When I tested a slow-learning class in which the children ranged in age from eleven to sixteen, hardly anyone could do the third drawing and a few had trouble doing the first one (Figure 24). Of course you can argue that these kids were not as smart as the kids in the regular class. That is true, but maybe they are not as smart because they could not do the drawings? "Anyhow it would be good if we could teach all the children in the slow classes to make the three-dimensional drawings. It may not make them geniuses but it can sure help," said their teacher.

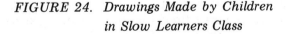

FIGURE 24. Drawings Made by Children in Slow Learners Class

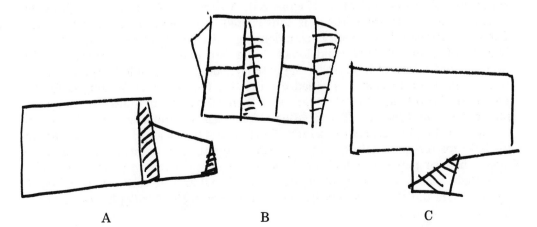

A   B   C

Do adults have space problems too? Space disabilities often follow a person to the grave. In adults the problem may not be too apparent because they tend to avoid the areas that involve space organization. Here is the typical comment of a person with a space problem: "I am not going to take the promotion because I hate the paper work," or "Let's tackle one thing at a time." This is an avoidance of detail work. For a person with good space organization, keeping track of details is not an overwhelming task. At one of our parents' meetings, an executive of a large company who tried and failed the drawing test laughed and said, "If it were not for my secretary, I would be in real trouble. She keeps me straight." A parent at the meeting for children with learning disabilities said, "Now we have the answer. If your child has a learning problem, get him a secretary!" If your school does not permit secretaries for children, get them some help and please do not call them Lazy Learners.

Internal Space

How do we help children who cannot draw? Probably the best thing we can do for these children is to *not* begin with drawing exercises. We teach them space. First, internal space. Can they tell where their arms and legs are located? By playing follow-the-leader, they can copy body postures—especially the Body Alphabet. Each letter of the alphabet has a pattern that can be made by the whole body. When the child learns where his limbs are located, we next teach him external space.

External Space

The *Flying Tiger Game* was devised to teach space. The basic principle of this game is to match a large pattern with a small pattern. The large pattern is negotiated by walking on a grid which is placed on the floor. The gross-motor experience is later translated into fine-motor pattern by drawing. The child is thus able to experience the form before he is asked to reproduce it.

SPACE TRAINING—FLYING TIGERS

Game 1—Pattern Reproduction

The object of this game is to improve form perception and retention. The main principle is to have the child remember lines drawn on a grid. In this game the grid is made by placing colored floor tiles in a prearranged pattern, six blue, one green, and one red. A large clear floor space is used and the tiles are placed approximately three feet apart (Figure 25). A series of three-by-five-inch cards, each bearing a different pattern, is constructed in preparation for the training. The cards increase in difficulty, commencing with two lines and progressing to five lines (Figure 26). The child looks at the card and walks the pattern on the floor. In order to add interest to the activity, the game is called Flying Tigers and the person directing it is called the Briefing Officer. The Briefing Officer shows the "flight plan" to the pilot who then "flies" a small airplane and places it on the final tile. The Briefing Officer has a drum which he will sound as soon as the pilot strays off course. This means that the pilot must return to his base for further briefing. After he has completed his flight, he is given a blank sheet of paper on which he draws his flight plan from memory. The pilot's flight plan is then compared with the original and he scores two points. If he has made the flight accurately but fails to match the flight plan on paper, he receives one point.

FIGURE 25. *Flying Tigers Floor Plan*

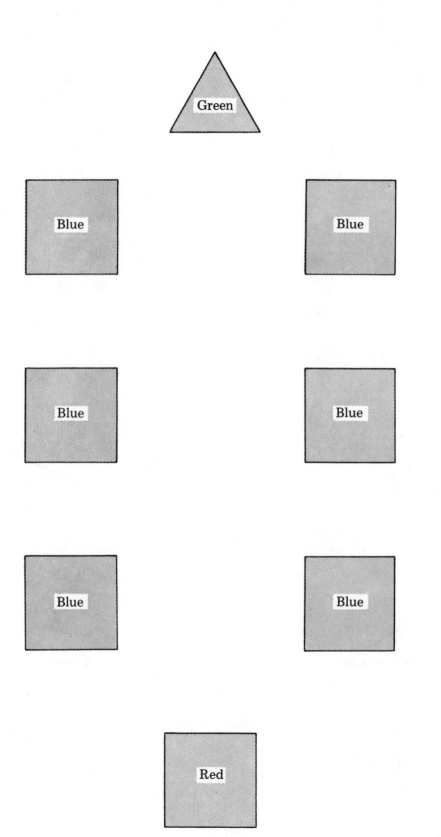

56

FIGURE 26. Flying Tigers Flight Plan

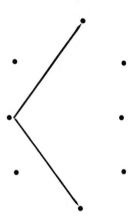

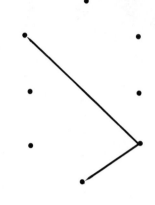

Level 1.

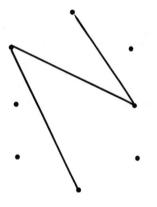
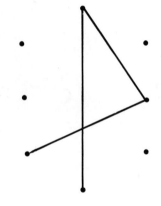

Level 2.

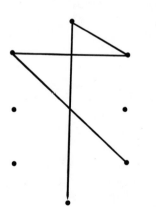

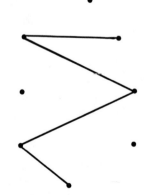

Level 3.

Game 2—Distance Estimate

This game is played in the same manner with the added requirement of estimating the number of heel-to-toe steps for each line. For example, after the child is given the first pattern, he must estimate how many steps he will take for the first line and the second line, then add the numbers and give the total. This will provide practice in both visual perception and number concept. After he has made the flight, he draws his flight plan and must record the difference between the measured and the estimated distance. Once the student has become familiar with the measurements for the standard three-feet distance between the tiles, the instructor changes the distance to four feet, five feet, and two and one-half feet.

Game 3—Visual Memory

The object of this game is to improve visual memory by flying "blind." After the pilot has checked his flight plan and is in position on the first tile, he is blindfolded and must negotiate the pattern from memory. He will be able to feel the slight elevation of the tile and thus develop tactual awareness in addition to visual memory. The drum is used to signal any error in flying.

These three games may be played as a pencil and paper task by children in the classroom. The teacher holds up the first pattern and the children copy the patterns on specially prepared pads where the grid has been previously drawn. For the distance estimate, a twelve-inch ruler may be used and the children would have to estimate the length of each line in inches. The third game, Visual Memory, is played by placing the pencil at the beginning tile, then closing the eyes and drawing the pattern.

EYE-HAND-MOUTH: THE FOUNTAINHEAD

This is a program for trainable and socially disturbed children. Sensorimotor training has had wide application for children with learning disabilities who were in the educable and normal range of intellectual functioning. What of the children who are lower on the scale? Children without language? Children without structure? Can sensorimotor training be instituted at that level? My experience with training at the eye-hand-mouth level has been very promising.

Authorities on child development have devoted considerable attention to the early motor patterns of the child. Jean Piaget, A. Gesell, Jerome Bruner, Burton L. White, R. Held and others have made careful observations of the first four months of child growth.[2] Bruner assigns a key role to the mouth as mediator for the eye-hand association: "At the outset, there is a growth . . . of attention that permits the child to register on salient object cues . . . . This development during the first three or four months involves not only the purely visual field, but also the orientation of the eyes, head, and body toward visual objects. Concurrently, the mouth becomes a kind of common terminus for both visual and manual-kinesthetic anticipation. The child learns to anticipate the approach of objects to the mouth. The mouth now becomes a kind of *tertium quid* between vision and manual movement . . . an anticipated goal response."[3]

I have attempted to develop this basic sequence by placing a food reward on a slowly rotating platform (Figure 27). The child must track the movement of the food with his eyes, then reach, grasp, and place the object in his mouth. The pleasure of the food reinforcement insures the continuation of the process.

*FIGURE 27. Eye-hand-mouth Training
for Grossly Retarded Children*

In a preliminary investigation of twelve children in the Children's Service Unit of the Douglas Hospital (Verdun, Quebec—a mental hospital), ranging in age from six to twelve with IQ range from 30 to 50, all the children were able to sustain a visual-manual pattern for ten to thirty minutes upon the very first application of the training.

A small room with bare walls, a table, and two chairs was the setting. The large rotating platform (Rotating Lazy Susan shown in Figure 27), with a speed of rotation between 10-20 rpm, is placed on the table and the therapist places a food reward on the rotating platform. The therapist uses a set verbal command for prelanguage children: "Johnny take the candy." The child usually responds by reaching for the moving candy and places it in his mouth. We were able to observe a number of different behaviors in this situation:

1. The child reaches out, seizes the candy with thumb and finger grasp, and places it in the mouth.

2. The child has difficulty in matching the speed of the moving target with his hand and moves his arm, shoulder, and trunk in search of his object.

3. The child opens his hand and tries to grasp the object with a palmer grasp (see Glossary). There is considerable force applied to the rotating platform in this maneuver.

4. The child stops the movement of the platform with one hand and retrieves the stationary candy with the other in a thumb-finger or a palmer grip. We had to restrain the arms of extremely hyperactive children when they approached the treatment area because of the threat to the apparatus. After the therapist had placed the food reward on the rotating platform and instructed the child, the restraints were removed and he immediately sought the candy.

A variety of rewards were used: fruit loops, raisins, M&M's, jelly beans, and peanuts. These effectively attracted the interests of the children. Later, the food reward was eliminated, and desired objects were substituted, such as small cars, colored blocks, beads, and coins. The moving targets proved to be motivating even at lower levels of reward. Thus, after the children had been trained with food reinforcers, they had developed sufficient visual-manual skill to operate at lower levels of motivation.

Developmental Significance

The eye-hand-mouth circuit is one of the most primitive behavior patterns. The establishment of integrity in this area may stimulate major changes in growth and development of exceptional children. We may have found a place to begin the rehabilitation of the majority of children who have failed to respond to the more traditional forms of therapy.

Vocational Training for Retarded Children

A plan for the application of this training principle for retarded teenagers and young adults has been made. A rotating platform that serves four trainees will be used for assembly work. The center rotating platform will bear four categories of objects. Each trainee will be responsible for retrieving one category of items. They will thus be given basic sensorimotor training that provides ocular tracking, eye-hand coordination, finger dexterity, and cognitive development (sorting) in one integrated and meaningful procedure.

REFERENCES

1. Jerome Bruner, *Eye, Hand and Mind: Studies in Cognitive Development* (London: Oxford University Press, 1969).

2. Jean Piaget, *The Origins of Intelligence in Children* (New York, N.Y.: International Universities Press, Inc., 1952); A. Gesell, *Infant and Child in the Culture of Today* (New York, N.Y.: Harper & Brothers, 1942); Bruner, *Eye, Hand and Mind*; Burton L. White, *Studies in Cognitive Development* (London: Oxford University Press, 1969); R. Held and J. A. Bauer, "Visually Guided Reaching in Infant Monkeys," *Science* (1967).

3. Bruner, *Eye, Hand and Mind*, p. 233.

Chapter 5. WHEN RIGHT IS WRONG OR HOW TO ELIMINATE REVERSALS

Why does a child have difficulty in telling his right from his left? Try this experiment: Be comfortably seated and write your name on the floor with your foot. Why did you select your right (left) foot? Now try the same task with the other foot. Is there a difference? Of course there is; the right (left) foot feels better or easier at the task. Can you remember the foot that first did the writing? Of course you can; it's the foot that feels easier. Why is the right foot easier? Is it because you practice? Not at all. One side of your body is more accomplished or skillful. What would happen to a child who couldn't feel any difference between his two sides? How would he ever remember which side he used? Answer: He can't because he has no reliable kinesthetic information. Watch the child as he goes about his daily activities. Sometimes he puts the chalk in his right hand and sometimes in his left hand. If one hand gets tired, he switches to the other. He does that because he feels no difference between his hands.

Now we shall try another experiment to understand reversals. Ask the child to close his eyes and, using both hands at the same time, write two letter c's on the chalkboard. Chances are one will be reversed. Try it yourself and chances are one will be reversed. Next ask him to draw two straight horizontal lines with both hands at the same time. Chances are one will be drawn in the opposite direction to the other. Why is that? Because man is a bilateral organism and symmetry is achieved by moving from the periphery of the body to the center. With the right hand the movement may be from right to left, and with the left hand it may be from left to right. Both hands are moving towards the center. Thus we can see that both movements are "natural" for the child. When the child does not have a consistent controlling side, he will make reversed movements when his control reference-point changes.

How to Teach Right and Left

The basic principle of the training is to create a kinesthetic awareness of one side through muscular fatigue. A three to five-pound weight (book, for example) is placed in the child's favored hand. He is asked to hold the weight in front of him for twenty seconds. This will produce an extreme fatigue in the muscle of one hand which will persist for twenty minutes. If the hand selected is the right hand, proceed as follows: "Show me your tired right hand. Using your tired right hand, touch your right foot. Using your tired right hand, touch your right knee. Using your tired right hand, touch your left shoulder," etc. This game may be played for five minutes. The positive kinesthetic referent helps to produce a confident and successful experience in laterality. This game can be played until the child can identify one side without any help. After five to ten practice periods, most children no longer need to use the weight. The mechanism of the tired side helps the child to attend to kinesthetic clues in a formal and controlled manner. Later he will use his new kinesthetic awareness to detect small differences in performance between his two sides, and he will thus establish reliable laterality and directionality.

How to Eliminate Reversals in Writing

Reversals in the primary grades are common. They are due to a lack of familiarity with the letter symbols as well as unstable laterality. Whichever cause is operating, the treatment is the same. Create a stable, reliable, self-administered system for writing the offending letters. Such a method came to mind when I examined Kenny, a nine-year-old boy who persistently reversed the capital *K* and *E* in his name. Using a blue index card, I cut a strip one inch by six inches and placed it on the left border of his writing page (Figure 28). A capital *K* and capital *E* were placed on the right side of the blue strip. He was told to use the strip as a ruler to draw the first line of the *K* and *E*. After drawing the first line, there was only one way to complete the letter and that was in the conventional direction. He practiced writing his name with the blue ruler ten times, and then he was able to work without any assistance.

FIGURE 28. *Making the First Stroke of "K" and "E"*
with a Cardboard Ruler

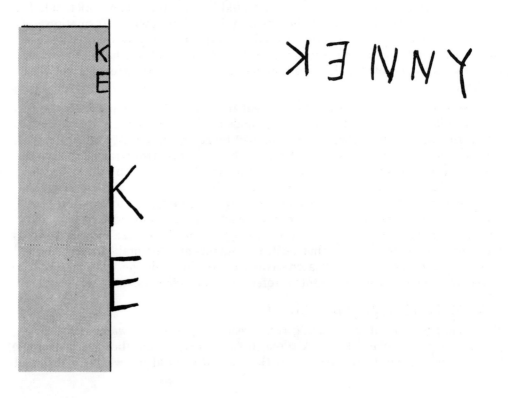

To help him solve the *b* and *d* dilemma, I made a pink cardboard ruler with a capital *B* placed near the right side of the strip and a capital *D* on the left side (Figure 29). He was asked to write the words *bee, boy, bat, bun, ball*, using his pink ruler on the side with the capital *B*. Next he was asked to write the words *dog, doll, dig, dam, ding*, using his pink cardboard ruler on the side of the *D*. After completing the *d*, he was asked to remove the ruler from his writing page and finish the word. Next he was given the words *bed, bad, bid, bud*, and he used the appropriate side of the ruler for each letter.

FIGURE 29. *Making the First Stroke of "b" and "d"*
with a Cardboard Ruler

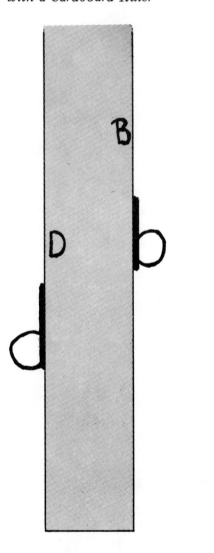

Using a different ruler, the *p* and *q* can be treated in the same fashion. It is unwise to teach more than one set of reversed figures at any one lesson. It is probably better to eliminate one set of reversals before tackling the second. When the *b-d* lesson has been learned and the child no longer requires the pink ruler, then the other reversals can be treated and eliminated one at a time.

Chapter 6. A CAUSE OF POOR READING IS POOR READING

A cause of poor reading is poor reading. This ambiguous statement may hold the key to a disability process that affects poor readers. Previously undetected, this general disability process interferes with remediation in reading and frustrates the efforts of dedicated teachers and often sets the stage for a lifetime of inefficient reading. This process is the linking of print with anxiety that can be described as a form of *print phobia*. The learning of anxiety follows the principles of classical conditioning described by I. P. Pavlov in 1927 and elaborated by Clark Hull and B. F. Skinner in learning theory. The basic statement of this principle is: event A and event B are experienced together. Later when event A occurs, then event B automatically emerges.[1]

An example of this process occurred with my niece. Barbara, age two, was recovering from a childhood illness and had fallen into a deep sleep. When she awoke, I approached her cot and picked her up. I was wearing my heavy dark-rimmed glasses, and in her state of disorganization, she reacted with unreasoned terror. Thereafter, whenever she saw me she would withdraw, especially if I were wearing my dark glasses. This fear did not manifest itself with strangers; it was specific to my person. She had linked event A, the quasi-real world of fever and general distress with event B, my person. Thus, whenever I appeared, she would immediately experience the emotional climate of event A.

PRINT PHOBIA

Let us look at a child with a reading disability from the point of view of classical conditioning. The preschool child does not have print phobia; print is one of a number of things in his environment that he has not yet become aware of, and his feelings about it can be described as neutral. But when he experiences his first reading lessons, he is—for many reasons—unsuccessful. He cannot make the desired response for his teacher. His first reaction may be one of deep embarrassment. He has failed not only in the eyes of his teachers, but in front of his peers. Event A, reading, becomes linked with event B, anxiety, frustration, embarrassment, a desire to withdraw that is socially unacceptable and is channelled into avoidance behavior. Thereafter, when he sees print (event A) the anxiety (B) returns inexorably and involuntarily. It is no longer a matter of will or motivation; he is powerless to undo the conditioned linkage in his nervous system. Physiological studies of the dyslexic child in the reading situation will show (1) increased blood pressure, (2) quickened heart and respiration rate, (3) hypertonicity of the voluntary and involuntary motor system, (4) cessation of the peristalsis of digestion, and (5) release of adrenalin in the blood system. This is the fight or flight process described by Walter B. Cannon, and the stress syndrome elaborated by Hans Selye.[2]

Anxiety and Perception

Although some anxiety or stress is required for alertness and involvement, a great deal of anxiety decreases the perceptual effectiveness of the individual. Compare the mild anxiety of the actor or the after-dinner speaker that sets the stage for a rousing performance, with the petrified, halting speech of the unprepared or unaccustomed speaker. In the first case, the mild anxiety produces an efficient performance; in the second case, the uncontrolled physiological storm disrupts the perceptual process.

Physiological studies of reading and anxiety were conducted by myself in collaboration with David Belanger, Director of the Institute of Psychology of the University of Montreal. They show marked decrease in perceptual ability (reading) with increased stress produced by reading acceleration.[3]

Thus we find the dyslexic child in a double bind; at the very time when he is reading and requires optimum functioning of his perceptual system, he is experiencing the involuntary anxiety linkage which further decreases his perceptual skill.

How can we break the linkage between print and anxiety? To get the answer we must turn to the behavior therapist. Albert Bandura provides a pertinent summary of the philosophy of behavior therapy: "Abnormal behavior can be thought of not as a symptom of a hidden illness, but as a problem of social learning and can be treated directly by means derived from the principles of learning."[4]

The neurotic response is inhibited when an incompatible pleasure-giving response is presented simultaneously. Let us see how this principle operates in a typical therapeutic situation for children who have a fear of dogs. A party setting is arranged where the children will have pleasurable responses, and then a film is shown in which a child is playing with a dog. During eight party sessions they watched a child interact closely with a dog. These children later lost their fear of dogs.

How Print Phobia Develops

Once children begin the reading experience, two main groups appear. The first group, whose experience has been positive, enjoy the lesson and look forward to more progress. The second group, whose experience has been negative, feel the frustration of falling further and further behind, come to the conclusion that they will never "catch up," and they begin the withdrawal of effort and affect. These groups represent the two extremes; beginners are placed along a continuum in their responses to reading. The old designation of a "mental block against reading" is probably a more accurate description of the process than is the more sophisticated modern terminology.

Mental Hygiene in Beginning Reading

One of the most sensitive periods in the child's school life is the first week of his reading experience. Many children enter this phase of their education with eyes bright and with eagerness to achieve, but this is short-lived when they cannot retrieve the sound of the symbol or the memory for the whole word—thereafter they become either able and positive or unable and negative. In much the same way, the primary-grade child dreads the gym if standards of performance are imposed too soon. To avoid the dangers of early failure in reading, it seems reasonable to proceed along two lines. The first is to sensitize the teachers to the meaning of the child's failure in relation to his peers, and second, to devise group training programs that enable the slow learner to remain anonymous while he is in the vulnerable period. During this period of anonymity, the number of reinforcements for each learned act should be increased by a factor of ten. Most beginning reading texts have between 8 and 15 reinforcements per word. The linguistic readers increase this to 30. The *Sesame Street* format employs 200 and more. The chief problem with massive reinforcement is to maintain the interest of the child.

Teachers Fail Beginning Reading

In order to sensitize the teachers to the meaning of failure, I asked a group of primary-grade teachers to learn a new alphabet. The Houghton Mifflin Company published an artificial alphabet to illustrate their principles of reading instructions. Following this idea, I used my own symbols, projected these lessons on the screen, and the teachers "read" the new words. Here is an example of the lessons.

WORDS	NEW ALPHABET
Sam	@+*
Daddy	)+))#
look	(??/
at	+%
me	*-
the	%$-
duck	)_½/
First Lesson:	(??/)+))# (??/ +% *-
Second Lesson:	@+* (??/ +% %$-)_½/

By the fifth lesson, the teachers were expected to read twenty-eight new words. The class as a group made excellent progress; they were able to decode all the words, but it was apparent from the responses of the teachers that there were great differences in the learning rate. However, all went well until I asked the teachers to read individually. One teacher became so flustered that she didn't notice that the translation appeared beside the word she was attempting to decode. They soon began to dread their turn and to experience the frustrations of the children in their own class.

THE NEW CURRICULUM

My next task was to construct a program for beginning reading that followed three principles: (1) the learner remains anonymous, especially from the teacher, (2) the reinforcements should be increased from 30 to 300, and (3) the teaching should be in the form of active games involving gross movement with a short period for seat work.

The curriculum: letter recognition, text from *Merrill Linguistic Readers*,[5] and writing.

The vehicle of instruction would be the following games: racing, basketball throw, tug of war, and Body Alphabet.

Materials: bean bags, Body Alphabet, charts, wastebasket, tracing paper, school desks, a whistle.

Experimental Class

To test the program, I asked the local school board to provide me with a class of twenty boys who not only had failed beginning reading but were unmotivated to learn and often caused disturbances in the class. The school district was in a mixed socioeconomic area. Many children in the school that we selected for the program were not encouraged by their parents to learn. They were often left to fend for themselves while both parents worked. A large number of children in this group were in the lower socioeconomic area. Some of the children came from a more advantaged background but they were not conforming to the class norms—either by withdrawing from the learning task or by creating a disturbance.

Since my purpose was to test the curriculum on a normal school population, I did *not* consult the children's school records. I did not know their intelligence status nor their health history. It soon became apparent when I began to work with them that many were perceptually handicapped and had motor and spatial difficulties. The program was not modified to suit the characteristics of any single child. The planning of the program assumed that difficulties would exist, but that the massive reinforcement, high motivation, and simplicity of the demands would enable them to perform satisfactorily. The goal was not only to teach reading, but to change attitudes to learning. If the new curriculum could succeed, then many current theories of the causes of reading and behavior difficulties would have to undergo serious revision.

The boys who were sent to this program belonged to the "print phobic group." They were not interested in learning to read; some were judged to be hyperactive, learning disabled, perceptually handicapped, borderline intelligence, culturally deprived, economically disadvantaged, and immature. Naturally, not all the children had the same degree of disability.

Teaching a class of boys outside of my accustomed clinical setting was a new experience for me. In my clinic we have a teacher-pupil ratio of one to three. I employ $30,000 worth of audiovisual and motor equipment. The children see cartoons, have a trampoline, build models, and eat ice cream. On the staff there are reading and speech therapists, special education consultants, and mature college students who work with the children. I wondered what I could accomplish with twenty-four dollars worth of Body Alphabet material, three dollars worth of bean bags, a plastic whistle, and a single linguistic reading textbook in a regular classroom.

Experimental Program Lesson Plan

Twenty boys were given four lessons per week of forty-five minutes each for a period of four weeks. My primary objective was to establish control of the class. To do this, we played the game of "freeze." The boys were permitted to run all over the classroom, but as soon as they heard the whistle they were to "freeze" their motion. If I wanted them to return to their seats, the signal was two whistle blasts. After they had learned to respond to the whistle, my program began with the Body Alphabet. Only those letters that were used in the first reader were taught in the order of the appearance of the words. They learned *h*, *a*, *t*, then *c* and *m*. They could make the words *hat*, *cat*, and *mat* with those letters.

The boys enjoyed moving around the room. On command they would make the posture for the letter *t*, then once again free movement was permitted, and after the whistle they were told to make the letter *m*, and so on for two lessons. In order to provide interest and accuracy, two boys were appointed as monitors. They each supervised nine boys—if one boy would make the wrong form for the letter or make a reversal, the monitor would throw a bean bag at the feet of the boy with the incorrect posture and the boy would immediately consult the chart and try to improve his posture. If he failed at this form of self-improvement, the monitor would correct him. Each day new monitors were appointed.

Reading New Words

The second objective, after I had achieved control of the group and taught them the letter names through the Body Alphabet, was to provide them with 300 reinforcements of the words *hat*, *cat*, and *mat*.

Game 1—Name and Touch

The children are divided into two teams—the reds and the blues—and they wear colored bands to identify their team. All the chairs and desks were swept to one side, with the exception of a line of chairs that separated the two teams (Figure 30). The red team members are the Namers while the blue team members are the Touchers. The chalkboard is divided into five panels. The three words are listed in each panel. This accommodates five children. The team members are numbered from one to ten. The first member of the Name team calls one of the words on the board—the Touch team is asked to volunteer for a chance to show the word on the chalkboard. If three children put up their hand, they are allowed to run to the board and touch the word. Three copies of each word are on the floor—protected by a plastic mat—and the children jump on the word as they run to the chalkboard. The idea of asking each member of the Blue team to take turns in calling a word, while the Red team *volunteers* to show it, is to protect the slow learner from error. While all could successfully call the words, even if they could not read them, only the most able children who could read these words would demonstrate their skill. This gives the slow learner an additional reinforcement without exposing him to failure. Within thirty minutes, all the children could read the words.

FIGURE 30. Name-and-Touch Reading Game

One member of blue team calls word.
Volunteer from red team runs to
chalkboard and touches word.

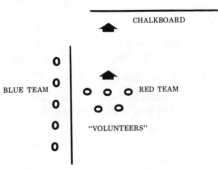

Game 2—Race and Touch

When all of the children could read the first three words, the setting was arranged for the Race (Figure 31). Each team has its own chalkboard. The referee calls the word *cat* and one member of each team runs to the chalkboard and touches all the *cats* on his board and steps on all the *cats* on the floor and then takes his place at the back of the line. The winners score a point for their team. Then the next boys in line have to find the word *mat*, and so on until each member has a turn. The children who are not running and touching words are reading every time a member of the team is in action, just to see if he is right. In this way it does not take long to cover 300 reinforcements.

FIGURE 31. *Race-and-Touch Reading Game*

Teams must step on word as they run
to chalkboard and touch word.

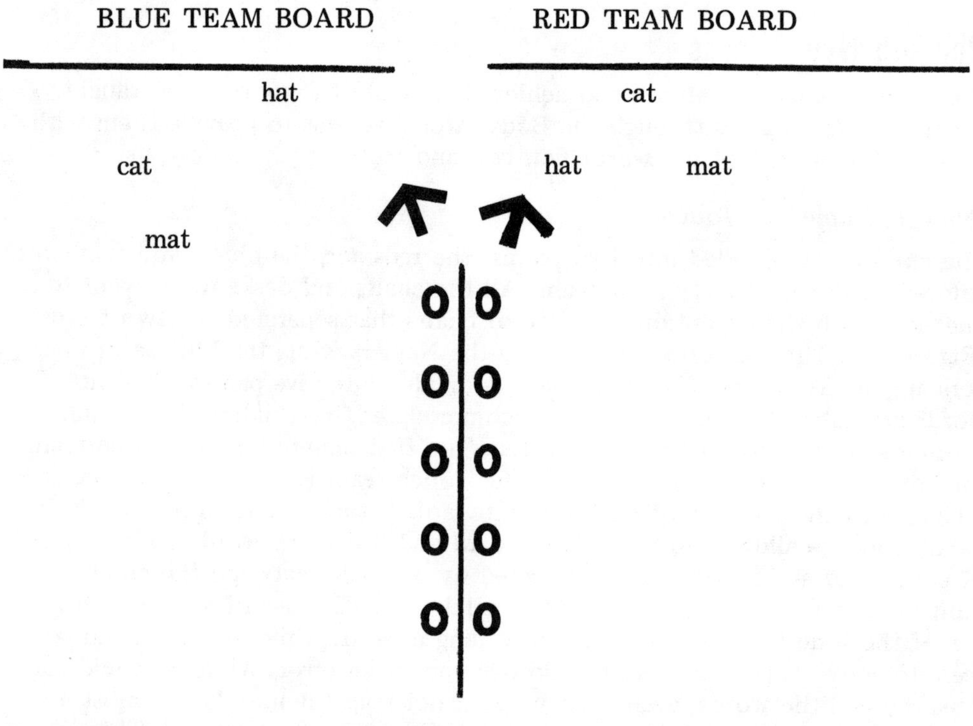

BLUE TEAM BOARD   RED TEAM BOARD

hat   cat

cat   hat   mat

mat

Thumbs Up — Thumbs Down

A quiet period of training should follow the active games. This is a good opportunity to teach listening. The beginning sounds can be taught in accordance with the principles of involvement and anonymity. Story Time helps the children sharpen their listening skills. When the story has achieved the objective of interesting the children, the game begins. Take a word from the story; for example, the word *boy*. Then tell the class, "I will go to the alphabet chart and touch some letters. When I am touching the first letter of the word *boy*, turn your thumbs up; if I touch the wrong letter, turn your thumbs down."

I introduce two sounds per day and base the examples on those sounds exclusively. For variety I ask for volunteers to go to the charts and touch the letters, while the class turns thumbs up or down. The children are asked to lie on the floor with their feet pointing to the chalkboard. There must be as much space as possible between the pupils in order to avoid distraction.

Writing New Words

To help prevent failure in writing, all the children trace the words on tracing paper. An arrow shows where to begin the letter and thus directionality is taught. In order to supply each child with his requirements for the lesson, a pencil and paper monitor was chosen for each lesson. The monitor would insure that each child had his supplies—each team had his own monitor.

Game 3—Bean Bag

The first twenty-one words of the textbook were stenciled so that each child had a stencil sheet with his course vocabulary, which was glued down on his desk. In order to play the bean bag game, the child had to write (trace) the first word, *cat*, ten times. If this was well done, he would receive a bean bag and be eligible for the game. Strict standards of tracing were demanded and achieved. The next word was *hat*. Words were chosen in random order; thus, the child had to read most of the words on the stencil as he searched for the required word. Those children who traced the ten words successfully formed into two teams and played the game (Figure 32).

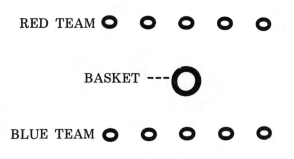

FIGURE 32. Floor Plan for Bean Bag Game

Children take turns tossing
bean bag into basket.

RED TEAM O O O O O

BASKET ---O

BLUE TEAM O O O O O

Independent Reading with Success

After the first twenty words were mastered (two new words were learned every day), the children were told that they could play Tug of War if they were to write (trace) ten words from their glued text and then *read them to me*.

Game 4—Tug of War

A one-half-inch rope, twenty feet in length, was made into a loop and used for this game. Those children who read their ten words were eligible to play. Members of opposing teams would try to pull their opponents across the center line.

Game 5—Snowball Fight Game

Each child wears a word on his chest (a word card is attached to a piece of string around his neck). The idea is to throw the snowball (crumpled paper ball) at the person whose word is called. Children stand on their chairs facing each other in their team formations ten feet apart. On the signal, red team throws the snowball at *mat*, and so on until each child has had his word read by the group (Figure 33).

FIGURE 33. Snowball Fight Game

Game 6—Take a Message

While each child is wearing his word, the instructor says, "I want the children wearing *cat-hat-mat* to go to the door and knock twice, then walk backwards to the basket and stand on the right foot." This increases auditory memory while the children read their words. The practice of asking three children to work together reduces the stress of failure and the less able children can follow the more dependable ones and get practice in understanding instructions. The instructions are varied each time: "The children wearing the words *bat-rat-sat*—ready, crawl to the teacher's desk, hop on two feet to the chalkboard and write your word, stand on your left foot," etc.

Game 7—Make a Word

The teams take their positions as in *Game 2*. The instructor says, "Red team make a word." The first three members of the red team go to the front of the room and make any word they want (form a Body Alphabet word) while the blue team reads it.

EVALUATION

The purpose of this study was not only to teach reading but to change attitudes to words in print. Most children who are placed in an unproductive situation re-act in the same way—they withdraw. The twenty boys in the group were selected because they failed beginning reading and had decreased their classroom participation in the reading activity.

Withdrawal from a task may be passive or active. The child who elects to use passive withdrawal retreats into a shell. He is characterized by his lack of communication and passivity—he rarely participates in discussion, does not move out of his seat, does not complete written assignments, and rarely disturbs other children or the teacher. The child who elects active withdrawal substitutes the lesson for irrelevant behavior; he shouts, moves from his seat, and scribbles on his workbook. It is expected that the most improvement would be observed in the passive group. The active group would not be expected to improve as rapidly because many have derived some satisfaction from being the center of the teacher's attention, even though it might be negative attention.

Of the twenty children selected for the program, ten were judged by their teachers as passive withdrawn and ten were disruptive (active withdrawn). After they had completed the four-week program, all the passive withdrawn children showed significant change in their classroom behavior. The school principal noted that many of these children seemed to move through the hallways in the school with new vigor and that they often talked about their new class. In the classroom the teachers reported that the passive children participated in discussions more often and did not require as much supervision for seat work. The teachers' observations are shown in Table 1.

TABLE 1. *Teachers' Observations of the Children After Completion of the Four-Week Program.*

PUPIL	BEHAVIOR PATTERN BEFORE PROGRAM		NO CHANGE	IMPROVED
	Withdrawn	Disruptive		
N.D.		•	•	
J.H.	•			•
J.K.		•	•	
B.M.		•		•
T.M.	•			•
N.N.		•	•	
P.T.	•			•
K.D.		•		slight
G.D.		•		•
S.N.	•			•
K.T.	•			•
G.C.		•		slight
J.HAL	•			•
J.C.	•			in math
G.B.	•			•
W.B.		•	worse	
C.B.	•			•
J.F.	•			•

Two children were not available for teacher comment.
One had left the school and the other was ill.

Summary

The ten passive children have shown improvement in their class work. Of the eight children who were disruptive, four showed some improvement, three showed no improvement, and one was worse. For these children, it is evident that a longer period of training would be required before the new behavior could be reinforced sufficiently for carryover to the regular classroom.

Teaching Skills

The teaching skills used in this program are more closely allied to the physical educator's work in team sports than to the traditional reading teacher's work. It seems logical to select teachers who can conduct these learning-game courses for all beginning readers for at least the first two months of the school year.

Some of the problems that were encountered in this program are inherent in any group situation; that is, the group activity is not always rewarding for all of the students all of the time.

I was fortunate in selecting games that had wide appeal, made few demands, and were enjoyed by most of the children all of the time. If this program were to be adopted by a school system for all primary-grade children, some children would not benefit from the activities because of severe motor, perceptual, or behavior disorders. These children would require a more individual approach in a quieter setting.

Curriculum Design

The following outline summarizes the program's goals and activites.

Gross-Motor Training	Races, Body Alphabet.
Fine-Motor Training	Tracing letters.
Body Image	Body Alphabet.
Reading Program	
Letter Recognition	Body Alphabet.
Merrill Linguistic Program	
Phonetics	Beginning and ending letter sounds from story hour.
Language Development	Games for following instructions.
Auditory Memory	Games with increasing number of instructions.
Visual Memory	Letter shapes.
Behavior	Only the desired behaviors were rewarded.

CONCLUSION

I have become aware of children with reading difficulties who have developed an anxiety linkage to print in accordance with the mechanisms described by Pavlov and others. The treatment of these reading disorders progresses more rapidly when the principles of behavior therapy are applied. Through the use of games, the *negative responses to print* are extinguished when a pleasure-giving situation is presented simultaneously.

Regardless of the method of reading instruction adopted—whether a linguistic, phonetic, or experiential approach is followed—the key factors in the situation are the teacher's sensitivity to the significance of early failure, and the child's need for anonymity while he is learning.

Further study is needed to develop curricula based on play activities inherent in the culture of the child so that the child can move from his play environment into the classroom without diminishing his excitement or joy.

REFERENCES

1. I. P. Pavlov, *Conditioned Reflexes* (London: Oxford University Press, 1927); C. L. Hull, *Principles of Behavior* (New York, N.Y.: Appleton Century Crofts, 1943); B. F. Skinner, *Science and Human Behavior* (New York, N.Y.: The Macmillan Company, 1953).

2. Walter B. Cannon, *Bodily Changes in Pain, Hunger, Fear and Rage* (New York, N.Y.: Appleton Century Crofts, 1920); Hans Selye, *Stress of Life* (New York, N.Y.: McGraw-Hill Book Company, 1956).

3. A. J. Kirshner, "Reading Training, 1945 to 1958" *Optometric Weekly* (September 17, 1959).

4. Albert Bandura, "Behavior Therapy," *Scientific American* (March 1967).

5. Charles C. Fries, Rosemary Wilson, Mildred K. Rudolph, *Merrill Linguistic Readers* (Columbus, Ohio: Charles E. Merrill Books, Inc., 1966).

Chapter 7. THEORIES

In this chapter you will find the theories: What is perception? Why does perceptual training help children to learn? What's wrong with Stimulus-Response learning theory? Answer: the middle is missing. And finally, a discussion of the basis of all child care—how to succeed with children by really trying!

OPTOMETRIC VISUAL TRAINING AND LEARNING DISABILITIES

The role of the optometrist in the treatment of learning disorders can be explained in terms of current learning theory by expanding the Stimulus-Response (S-R) formula. The current focus of the learning theorists is on the stimulus and the response. Treatment procedures are devised that follow each correct response with a reward that is either social (praise) or material (token). Impressive gains have been made with this methodology in the treatment of many types of exceptionality in children and adults.

The operant conditioning principles of B. F. Skinner, and the work of E. L. Thorndike and I. P. Pavlov have provided the theoretical framework of behavior therapy,[1] but the focus of the therapist on the stimulus and the response has diverted the attention away from a significant area of investigation—the organism itself. If we expand the S-R formula to the earlier model of Thorndike, it becomes S-I-R. "I" stands for integration. Investigating the events that occur during the time between the stimulus and the response may yield benefits for the slow learner. This is precisely the area in which the optometrist has been working. Improvement of ocular tracking, focusing, binocularity, body image, eye-hand coordination, and audiovisual-motor integration, led to better organization of neural nets that could significantly reduce the time between stimulus and response for decoding symbols and manipulating numbers.[2]

What Is Perceptual-Motor Training?

What is perception and how does movement improve it? Instead of adding yet another definition to an overburdened literature, I shall share an experience with the reader that will link three states of mind—sensorimotor, perception, and cognition. Each of these three mental states will become clear as you slowly turn the pages. A picture will emerge as you go from page to page (Figures 34-38). Your task is to note the page number that provides you with your first clue; that is, the identification of one part of the picture. Next, note the page that gives you the full comprehension of the picture. As the meaning emerges, you will pass through the three stages—sensorimotor, perception, and cognition. The characteristics of each stage will be discussed, and later we shall see how movement assists the preperception stage of sensorimotor organization.

Experience in giving this demonstration to hundreds of persons shows that the majority of viewers identifies the first meaningful part of the picture at the third page (Figure 36), and the total meaning at the fifth page (Figure 38). We now have a common experience upon which to base our definitions. The sensorimotor stage is page one and two (Figures 34-35)—the characteristics of this stage are (1) attention to visual data, (2) scanning or eye movements, but (3) there is no meaning. The perception stage is reached on page three (Figure 36) when the viewer recognizes one element of the picture story. The characteristics of this stage are (1) the grouping of selected parts, and (2) the relating of this grouping of parts to past experience. Another way of stating this is to say that parts of the visual field are cemented and that this newly cemented figure is matched with past experience. The cognitive stage is achieved when three perceptions (percepts) are integrated and then related to past experience (Figure 38). The characteristics of the cognitive stage are (1) the grouping of selected percepts and, (2) matching this grouping with past experience. (See following pages.)

Perceptual and Cognitive Disorders

There are two possible sources of perceptual disorder in children:

1. When the child fails to group or cement the parts of a form.
2. When the child cannot relate a pattern to past experience.

When the first disorder occurs, we say that the child has a perceptual handicap. When the second is the case, we say that the child has an experiential void. Many children in the Head Start program have communication disorders which stem from the experiential void—they lack sufficient symbols for their school environment.

Children with learning difficulties may have disorders that are the result of a failure in "grouping" data or matching sensory data with past experience. It is the former type of disorder that has been the main area considered in this book —although it will readily be seen that children from deprived environments may have both disabilities. Thus, this book may be useful in offering remediation for the environmentally deprived child if the activities are interwoven with experience and language training.

LEARNING THEORY AND LEARNING DISABILITIES

E. L. Thorndike, Ivan Pavlov, and B. F. Skinner have made a significant contribution to understanding the learning process of normal children. The stimulus-response formula based on the studies with Thorndike's cats, Pavlov's dogs, and Skinner's pigeons was less successful in treating children with learning disabilities. The reason for this is that they used normal animals in their research. Of much greater significance for the child with the learning problem are

FIGURE 34.

FIGURE 35.

FIGURE 36.

FIGURE 37.

FIGURE 38.

the animals of R. Held (kittens), W. R. Thompson (scotch terriers),[3] D. Kretch (rats),[4] and A. H. Riesen (chimpanzees).[5] These animals suffered some restrictions in their early development in movement or in light. They were inferior to their litter mates in problem solving, spatial orientation, and they showed a lack of ability to discriminate relevant from irrelevant aspects of their environment. To improve the learning status of these animals, they required motor experience to explore their environment (Held, kittens). Many animals never caught up to their peers; they required many more trials for learning and were generally less able. In order to understand the behavior of the learning-disabled animals, it was necessary to study the events that occurred between the stimulus and the response.

Motor Planning

One of the events that occurs between the onset of the stimulus and the resulting behavior is organizing the mechanism for movement. Some idea of the complexity of this mechanism can be had by studying the movement of the eyes. It will be shown, that in the improvement of the eye movement, large areas of the brain are organized.

When a child follows a moving target with his eyes there are two processes at work.

1. He must detect the direction and speed of the movement.

2. He must transmit this information to the eye muscles so that the center of clear vision of each eye may remain on the moving target. The research of Hubel at Harvard has shown that the cells in the visual receptive area are highly specialized in their behavior.[6] By studying the action of single cells to the direction of a line, he found that these cells were specialized. One cell could detect only a horizontal line and no other. Some cells could detect diagonal lines while other cells only detected vertical lines. You can readily see how much organization was needed to pick up the information from each of these specialized cells to determine the direction of the moving target. The second stage which was following the target with the eyes was investigated by Irving Wagman, University of California.[7] He found evidence, similar to Hubel's, that cells were specialized in the way in which they moved the eyes. Some moved the eyes horizontally, others in a vertical and diagonal direction. If the proper sequence of cells were fired the eyes would stay on the moving target, but if these cells were not organized as is the case with children with perceptual-motor difficulties, an improper sequence of cell firing would occur and the eye would veer away from the target. How can these children play baseball or read without losing their place?

To understand the therapy which consists of repetitive movement patterns, we must look at the way individual neural cells communicate. There is no direct contact between cells. The impulse from one cell to another takes place when there is sufficient chemical transmitter present. In order for a particular sequence of cells to synchronize their action, an enriched supply of chemical transmitter substance must be developed along the desired path. With repeated practice of a movement, tiny knobs develop which supply the substance. David Kretch and his coworkers have shown that mice reared in isolation showed less brain weight and lower concentration of chemical transmitter substance than the litter mates who were given perceptual-motor experiences. When the educator asks how does trampoline and eye-movement training improve reading, the answer is: only reading can improve reading, but motor based therapy can reduce the delays and the frustrations in keeping the eye on the track. It may have another influence which is just as profound. Although the exact mechanism is not clear, the cementing of the neural cells produce controlled movement which parallels the cementing of visual elements into patterns that are related to past experience (perception). D. O. Hebb speculated that the relation of the eye movement to visual perception was like the hand on the builder, "lines and angles can be treated as perceptual elements and the eye movement as the hand of the builder."[8] Go back to the pictures of the children on the see-saw (pages 79-83). Notice as you turn the pages that the form emerges as you "cement" various shapes into a form that can be related to past experience. You will see that the uniting action is the exploratory eye movement.

I recall vividly the bright, articulate, high school student, who was unable to learn geometry before his perceptual-motor training, exclaim, "Now I can see the three triangles for the first time." His reaction to figure perception after gross-motor and fine-motor training, shows the spontaneous nature of the gestalt process (Figure 39). He was not given any training in geometry during his four-month rehabilitation program.

The key concept of this book is that children who are slow learners and poorly coordinated, either in gross or fine movement, require a movement based therapy preceding or concomitant with academic help.

FIGURE 39.

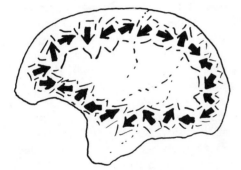

Unorganized sensorimotor cells produce incoordination

Fragmented form perception

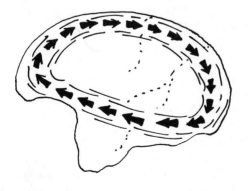

Organized sensorimotor cells produce skilled movement

Stable form perception

HOW TO SUCCEED WITH CHILDREN BY REALLY TRYING

Since the purpose of this book is to help parents and teachers help children with learning disabilities, it seems fitting to review the factors that have made for success in our clinic.

How I Discovered the Role of the Teacher

Few students looked forward to professional practice in optometry with as much eagerness as I did. I had devoted a considerable amount of time to the study of visual training. I had purchased the latest equipment. I attended seminars and workshops on the techniques of visual training. The training was meticulously applied in my office. The first disappointment I experienced was when children failed to finish their program. It was difficult for the parents to get them to attend. Even more devastating was the blow that 90 percent of the patients I had trained did not return to the office. They had chosen other practitioners. I carefully reviewed my training procedures. For eye movements I employed an instrument that consisted of a twenty-inch disc with a red bicycle reflector mounted near the rim. A variable speed motor was used to rotate the disc while the patient looked at the rotating reflector. Fifteen minutes of eye-movement training in the form of rotations was given in this way. The objective was to improve the tracking mechanism of the eyes. The next objective was to improve the flexibility of focusing. In order to do this I employed lenses of varying powers and asked the patient to look at a reduced Snellen chart held at fourteen inches. He was instructed to try to see clearly as I changed the lenses. Eye-hand coordination was taught by having the patient place two pickup sticks on various points of a picture seen in a stereoscope. If the eye-hand relationship was poor, the patient would improve it by trying to touch the target. To improve depth perception I employed stereograms (three-dimensional pictures) viewed in a stereoscope. Pictures that were graded from "easy" to "difficult" were viewed by the patient until he could report the depth in a target with a very small amount of retinal disparity. Fusion training to improve two-eyed vision and eliminate blocking of vision or suppression in one eye was given by chieroscopic drawing. The instrument for this training is basically a stereoscope with a platform for holding a picture and a pad of drawing paper; it helps eliminate suppression in this way: the patient sees the picture with the left eye and he traces the picture with a pencil held in the right hand, seen only with the right eye. At first the patient reports that the picture (left suppression) or the pencil (right suppression) fades while he is tracing. Later he notes that both picture and pencil are seen at all times.

For eight years I followed this curriculum, and I was thoroughly discouraged about ever succeeding with patients in visual training. I attended seminars and returned with a glow of enthusiasm, only to fail once more. It was then that Jimmy came to my office, and I made a decision that was to change his life and mine: his training was based on sound physiological principles, but it had to be brought to life. That meant that all the demands of the training had to be translated into meaningful activities for the child. To make the eye-movement training more meaningful, I gave Jimmy a dart gun and said, "Jimmy, let me see you hit that moving red reflector." This was the first time that a patient of mine had a basic desire for looking at the rotating target. His attention span increased; I found that I could keep patients playing this game because they enjoyed target shooting. The next change came in the focusing flexibility training. I substituted a *Batman* comic for the reduced Snellen card. Now the patient quickly changed focus in order to see the pictures and read the captions.

For eye-hand coordination I used model building. Here was a challenging situation for fingers and mind. The drawing in the stereoscope was enhanced by asking the child to trace favorite comic characters. To train depth perception, I rigged up a bomber on a string and had the patient pull the airplane along the string until he was over the target, then he would release the bomb. He soon learned to judge space and distance. Absenteeism was eliminated completely by this means. Now I was faced with a new problem: children did not wish to graduate from the program.

Creating programs for the high school student was very challenging. The example of Jules, age sixteen, is typical of the approach I have employed. Jules was in grade ten, and he had never repeated a grade. He was always a borderline student, he did not distinguish himself in athletics, and he had few friends. His major difficulty in school was reading and composition. The sensorimotor examination showed that he had an oculomotor difficulty, and his writing was below the standards for his age. I decided that he would benefit from visual training and remedial reading. His attitude, however, was quite negative. He wanted to quit school. He had few hobbies and he would sit home every night and weekends. The parents were understandably concerned. During the examination, Jules was reticent and resentful about being examined. He did not respond to the suggestion of model building or electronic construction projects. In my interview with the parents I had learned that Jules was an avid hockey fan, that he had volunteered the previous summer for playground assistant, and that he liked to work with children.

It was clear from his attitude that Jules would not respond to the idea of taking remedial reading or attending training sessions to improve his visual skills. I tried very hard to make the training relevant and used my knowledge of his interests to suggest a program. "How would you like to be a sports reporter?" I asked. "That's terrific," he responded. I pointed out that a sports reporter could get in free to all the games and he could be a sports personality. In order to carry out his objective, he would have to follow the path of a newspaper worker. He would have to find a job on a newspaper—distribution, rewriting, interviewing, or even office work. He would have to get this experience on his school newspaper. He promised to apply for the job of sports reporter on his high school paper, but he would take any job that was offered. The next step in his journalistic career would be to learn photography—since the reporters had to shoot their stories. He agreed to this step and bought a kit to develop and print his own pictures. Next, he recognized the need for typing. I told him that at our office he could study journalism. Our reading teacher would show him the formula that all writers used:Who, Where, What, When, Why. If he could answer these questions, he would get a complete story as he followed a robbery or questioned a rich society patron about the entry of her famous dog in the dog show. In addition to taking the course in journalism, he could help out as model-building assistant for our younger patients. He would receive an assistant's salary for any work he performed in our clinic.

Jules' parents were delighted with his new-found enthusiasm. They helped him purchase the photo kit and rented a typewriter so that he could practice at home. Jules applied for work on the school paper and was accepted. Later, he became the manager of the hockey team and his writing in the school paper was not below the standards of writing for the school. His work in the clinic was excellent; he mastered the skills before teaching the children, and in this way he was eager to take the visual training. In discussing my successes with these children, it is not my intention to criticize classroom teachers, nor to suggest that the teachers are not interested in their profession, nor that they are doing inferior work. Far from it, the art of teaching demands a special kind of empathy and sensitivity in the interaction with the student. It is not in the face-to-face situation with the student that the "trying" must take place, but in the preparation to make the curriculum relevant—this is where the effort should be applied.

CONCLUSION

I have had rich experiences in helping children because I have given priority to the sensorimotor status of the child and have tried to make the curriculum relevant. Opening the channels of communication by sensory training, developing the responsive functions of the organism through skilled movement, and finally, integrating all the sense modalities through rhythmic movement patterns visually directed, will not only increase the effectiveness of children who are not meeting the demands of daily life, but will enhance and enrich the lives of children who are meeting the standards set by the community.

REFERENCES

1. B. F. Skinner, *The Behavior of Organisms* (New York, N.Y.: Appleton Century Crofts, 1938); I. P. Pavlov, *Conditioned Reflexes* (London: Oxford University Press, 1927); E. L. Thorndike, *Animal Intelligence* (New York, N.Y.: The Macmillan Company, 1911).

2. A. Silver and R. Hagan, "Perceptual Training," *Journal of Ortho Psychiatry* (Summer 1967).

3. W. R. Thompson and W. Herron, "The Effects of Restricting Early Experience on the Problem Solving Capacity of Dogs," *Canadian Journal of Psychology*, 8 (1954), 17-31.

4. David Kretch, E. L. Bennett, M. C. Diamond, and M. R. Rosensweig, "Chemical and Anatomical Plasticity of Brain," *Science*, 164, (October 1964), 610-619.

5. A. H. Riesen and L. Gans, "Stimulus Generalization to Hue in Dark Reared Macaque," *Journal of Comparative and Physiological Psychology*, 55 (1962), 92-99.

6. D. H. Hubel and T. N. Wiesel, "Receptive Fields and Functional Architecture in the Cat's Visual Cortex," *Journal of Physiology*, 160 (1962) 106-154.

7. Irving H. Wagman, *Oculomotor Systems* (New York, N.Y.: Harper and Row, 1964).

8. D. O. Hebb, *Organization of Behavior* (New York, N.Y.: John Wiley & Sons, Inc., 1949).

APPENDIX

RELATIONSHIPS BETWEEN KIRSHNER SENSORIMOTOR SCALE AND MEASURES OF ACHIEVEMENT AND COGNITIVE DEVELOPMENT

A significant relationship exists (r's significant to .01 level) between the Kirshner Sensorimotor Scale and *Wechsler Intelligence Scale for Children* (WISC), *California Achievement Tests*, and Piaget's Right-Left Awareness Test.

WISC	.525*
PIAGET	.703
READING	.469
MATH	.565

*Pearson Product Moment Coefficient

The relationship between sensorimotor levels and cognitive development has been described by L. L. Emerson.[1] Experiments involving perception and movement in young children showed that when the children were asked to retain concrete perceptual relationships after hopping to the corner of the room and back before placing a ring in its proper relationship, the three-year-old children were completely disrupted by the process. The older children were not affected by this motor interlude. It would therefore seem reasonable to conclude that children who do not have adequate sensorimotor development are more likely to delay reaching the Piaget stage of concrete operations. This notion is supported by the data.

MATURATIONAL DEFICITS AND LEARNING IN THE YOUNG CHILD

S. A. Dudek, A. J. Kirshner, and E. P. Lester, in collaboration with
R. C. Muir, J. Goldberg, and E. Bloom. Educational Research Council.

The research area in which we have concentrated has been in the field of maturation of cognitive, conceptual (Piaget), perceptual-motor and personality (ego adequacy) functioning, and the relationship of these variables to the development of stability in early academic learning.

Subjects: 107 children, ages 5.0 to 6.3, attending kindergarten at two Protestant public schools. They were from a homogeneous socioeconomic background (income $7,500—$10,000). There were 53 girls and 54 boys. Children below 80 IQ were excluded from the study.

These children were followed longitudinally from kindergarten through elementary school (September 1966 to June 1969) in an attempt to establish criteria based on early test measurement for predicting later school achievement. The Kirshner battery was administered in 1968-69 when the children were 7—8.3 years old. The following were among the tests given:

Weschler Intelligence Scale for Children (WISC)

Rutgers Drawing Test

Lincoln Oseretzsky Motor Development Scale

Psychiatric Scale: The psychiatrists attached to the study used a structured interview questionnaire consisting of studies of the following maturational hazards: (1) emotional stress in the family, (2) severe illness in a parent or child, and (3) physical absence of a parent.

Kirshner Sensorimotor Scale: Measures of motor development and sensorimotor integration.

California Achievement Test (Academic Achievement)

Laurendeau Pinard Tests of Piaget Preoperational/Operational Intelligence in the Child

The *Kirshner Sensorimotor Scale* measures: (1) Ocular control, (2) Eye-hand coordination, (3) Head control, (4) Handwriting rate, and (5) Sensorimotor integration with arrows and hand prints.

1. OCULAR CONTROL:

A QUANTITATIVE MEASURE OF EYE MOVEMENTS

Optometrists are interested in the quality of ocular movements and observe this skill as a part of their investigation into the structure and function of the human eye. Recording of the observations of eye-movement skill is descriptive. Thus eye movements are designated as smooth, irregular, or erratic under the conditions of the test. Circular pursuits, principal meridian tracking, monocular and binocular activities are all observed, and the quality of the movement is noted on the test form.

APPARATUS

The apparatus employed to investigate the eye movements is a rotating mirror and a Snellen Projector. The mirror is mounted to a variable speed electric motor by means of a ball and socket hinge or universal joint. This permits the mirror to be angled with respect to the axis of rotation of the motor shaft. The range of speeds is between 10 and 100 RPM. The target size is 20/40. The distance of the patient from the screen is 10 feet and the diameter of rotation of the target on the screen is 4 feet. The angle with the nodal point of the eye is 21 degrees. The Snellen slide is reversed so that when projected onto a plate glass mirror, the letters are seen in their normal orientation.

ADMINISTRATION OF TEST INSTRUCTIONS TO PATIENT

"I am going to test your eye movements. Efficient eye movements are important for reading, for driving, for sports, and many other visual tasks. Do you see the letter moving on the screen? I shall soon increase the speed of the moving letter to a point where you cannot see it. It will be moving too quickly; then I shall change the letter and gradually slow it down until you can recognize it. As soon as you recognize the first letter, I shall keep changing the letters and you must read them as soon as you can. Please do not move your head or body while taking the test." When the patient can read 4 consecutive letters, the speed in rpm is recorded.

MOTOR SUPPORT

It is important to note the motor support that the patient exhibits while performing the eye-movement test. When the eye movements are unreliable and inefficient, the patient will break the "Law of Parsimony" and call upon head rotation to support the ocular tracking movements. Often in extreme cases of eye movement disability, the patient will move his trunk. Designating the amount of motor support is thus an important part of the eye-movement evaluation. An assistant can be trained to make the motor support observations while the optometrist attends to the instrument and the accuracy of the patient's responses. Motor support is judged on the following five-point scale:

M-1: No head movement.

M-2: Transient head movements.

M-3: Constant head rotations at target speed.

M-4: Transient head and trunk movements.

M-5: Constant head and trunk movements linked to target.

2. EYE-HAND COORDINATION TEST:

The patient holds a pointer flashlight that projects a small arrow on the screen. He is requested to keep the arrow on the moving target. The target is the open slot on the AO projector with the red-green filter. It measures 11" square. Distance from the screen is 10 feet, diameter of rotation is 4 feet.

INSTRUCTIONS TO PATIENT

"I am going to test your eye-hand coordination. You must keep the arrow in the red-green square as I gradually increase the speed. Move your arm only. Do not move your body." For junior patients, "Let us pretend that I have a moving spaceship; you have the astronaut (arrow). You must keep the spaceman in the spaceship." Allow two minutes for practice; alternate the use of the hands. The subject must keep the arrow on target for 3 successive revolutions. Begin at a low speed and increase. Test dominant and subdominant hand.

MOTOR SUPPORT

Patients with poor eye-hand coordination will hold the arm rigidly and rotate the trunk. Patients with splinter skills will hold the arm rigid and move only the wrist and hand. The expected performance is a smooth arm movement with minimum trunk rotation. Motor support is judged on the following five-point scale:

M-1: Arm movement with slight trunk rotation.

M-2: Wrist movement alone.

M-3: Arm movement with transient body support.

M-4: Arm movement with fused trunk support.

M-5: Wiggle. Children below age 5 who cannot relate the arm movement to the target will extend the arm and wiggle the light or move up to the screen in an effort to touch the target.

3. HEAD CONTROL

Head control plays an important role in directing body movement. The head and trunk are linked at birth through the tonic neck reflex.

INSTRUCTIONS TO THE PATIENT

The Burgess Headlight is adjusted so that it projects the beam of light at eye level when the head is held erect. The patient is asked to keep the light on the moving red-green target. The highest speed at which the patient can maintain the light on the target for 3 consecutive rotations represents the score.

MOTOR SUPPORT

This again is judged on a five-point scale. The expected performance is smooth rotation of the head without trunk movements. Patients with inadequate movements use the muscles of the back and chest to assist the head movement.

M-1: No trunk support. Head movements are smooth.

M-2: Head movement with transient trunk support. Slight irregularities in head movement are noted.

M-3: Consistent trunk rotations at target rotation speed.

M-4: Transient body shift. The lower limbs and the trunk are involved. Interruptions in head movement can be observed.

M-5: Vertical oscillation of the head and trunk movements. Patient cannot relate his own movements to the target.

4. DYNAMIC HANDWRITING TEST:

This test measures the writing speed. The rate of writing is related to achievement and indicates the degree of freedom in the writing process. Students who have slow writing rates experience difficulty in expressing themselves in this medium. They are far better at oral tests. Writing is often judged by form alone. This is an incomplete measure because a poor writer will show an improvement in his writing by working slowly and increasing the pressure; however, under the stress of carrying out a classroom assignment, his fine handwriting quickly deteriorates. For the nursery, kindergarten, and grade 1 students the writing test consists of making circles at high speed. For grade 2, the alphabet is used. The students are urged to make as many letters as possible in 30 seconds. The test is repeated for the opposite hand. For grade 3, age 8 and up, the test consists of spelling the numbers. The number of units produced in 30 seconds represents the score.

5. SENSORIMOTOR INTEGRATION TESTS:

VISION, AUDITORY, GROSS-MOTOR DIRECTIONALITY TEST

Place the Arrows chart at eye level, three feet from the student. Set the metronome at 60 and ask student to point in the direction of the arrows as he names directions: up, down, right, and left.

INSTRUCTIONS

"Please count the arrows on the chart. While you count them show with your hand the direction in which they are pointing. Listen to the metronome and count in time with the beat. If you count exactly on the beat, you will get a high score." Demonstrate test and exaggerate precision with which the voice and metronome blend. After a short practice period, score percentage correct for 36 arrows. Use tape recorder to assist in scoring.

VISION, AUDITORY, FINE-MOTOR SPEECH TEST

Place Fingers chart at eye level, three feet from the subject. Set the metronome at 60 and ask subject to make the finger patterns as he tells how many fingers he sees in each pattern (thumb is counted as finger). He must arrange his fingers in the desired pattern to each beat of the metronome. Repeat for nondominant hand. Score percentage correct out of 20. Subject receives 50 percent for being able to make the finger patterns without looking at his hand even though he may not be able to keep the metronome pace.

REFERENCES

1. L. L. Emerson, "Body Orientation and Meaning," *Child Development*, 2 (1930), 125-142.

GLOSSARY OF TERMS

BINOCULAR VISION: The faculty of superimposing the two central images of the retinae and projecting them into space as a single image.

ELECTRO-OCULOGRAM: A method of studying the ocular movements by recording the electrical activity associated with movement of the eyes. Electrodes are placed on the skin surface near the eye and the quality of the movements can be observed on the recording instrument.

HYPERTONICITY: When a muscle is at rest, there is a constant level of activity in the muscle known as *tonus*. When the degree of activity is higher than average, the condition is referred to as hypertonicity.

INTERMODAL INTEGRATION: The ability to translate information from one sensory mode to another. For example, the international Morse code can be identified as a system of auditory input which is matched with an equivalent visual pattern. The sound ("dit dit dah") can be matched with the visual symbols (. . —). The research of H. Birch and L. Belmont has linked efficiency of intermodal function with learning disabilities.

LOG ROLLING: Barrel rolling without a barrel. The hands are placed by the sides and the child rolls on the floor.

MODALITY: The dictionary defines "modal" as indicating a mode, a way, method, or form. A visual, auditory, motor, kinesthetic, tactual, olfactory, or gustatory form of behavior.

OCULAR CONTROL: A. Gesell and his coworkers have noted that the infant establishes ocular control within the first four weeks of life. Ocular control refers to the ability of the child to follow a moving target with his eyes.

OCULOMOTOR SKILLS: The ability to locate and follow a moving target is accomplished by the ocular muscles. The efficiency of these eye movements can be increased by specific training.

OPTOMETRIC EXTENSION PROGRAM: An optometric postgraduate organization founded by A. M. Skeffington and E. B. Alexander. It is a worldwide organization of optometrists devoted to maximizing human performance through the employment of lenses, prisms, and movement.

OPTOMETRIC VISUAL TRAINING: The employment of lenses and prisms with motility training of eyes, and eyes, hands, and body in space. This form of training, when given to children with visual problems related to learning, is often called Developmental Training because the sequences follow the stages of child development.

PALMER GRASP: A primitive infant grasp observed very early in life. This develops to the more refined use of the hand that requires the finger and thumb opposition.

PERCEPTUAL-MOTOR TRAINING: The purpose of perceptual-motor training is to enhance the learning ability of the child. Either maturational lag or injury to the nervous system can bring about impaired performance in movement and sensory awareness. A systematic program of developing the early movement patterns of ocular control and locomotion linked to tactual, auditory, and visual modes forms the core of this program.

PERISTALSIS: A rhythmic contraction of the intestinal tract associated with digestion.

PLUS LENSES: A convex lens which, when used under certain conditions, enhances such near-centered tasks as reading and fine assembly work.

RED GLASS DRAWING: A method of eliminating suppression of vision in one eye. Suppose that the left eye periodically blocks or suppresses its image. The optometrist will try to arrange conditions in which the patient can detect the suppression and overcome it. By placing a red glass before the right eye and asking the patient to draw pictures on a white paper with a red pencil, the line is visible by the left eye alone. The red glass transmits both the white paper and the red pencil strokes without contrast, and the line is therefore invisible to the right eye. The patient will be forced to rely entirely on his left eye for the information while keeping the right eye employed in seeing under binocular conditions.

SENSORIMOTOR: Refers to the integration between the input (sensory) and output (motor) modes of behavior.

SENSORIUM: Describes the relationships between the gustatory, olfactory, kinesthetic, auditory, and visual modes of behavior.

SPACE AWARENESS: M. D. Vernon states, "The only information that we get from the outside world is relative." We see and respond to objects in relation to other objects. These relationships are maintained through the development of a space structure. N. C. Kephart states that a person with a stable space structure is said to have space awareness.[1]

REFERENCES

1. M. D. Vernon, *A Further Study of Visual Perception* (New York, N.Y.: Cambridge University Press, 1957); N. C. Kephart, *Slow Learner in the Classroom* (Columbus, Ohio: Charles E. Merrill Books, Inc., 1960).